RAISING KIDS WHO BLOSSOM

Priceless Parenting For Healthy Growth

Kathy Slattengren, M.Ed.

Priceless® Parenting

Priceless Parenting® LLC
www.PricelessParenting.com
425-770-1629

Copyright © 2018 by Kathy Slattengren, M.Ed.

Originally published in 2009. Revised editions in 2010, 2013, 2014, 2018.

Cover and Interior Design: Kathy Slattengren

Printed in the USA

All rights reserved. No part of this book may be reproduced in any form without permission in writing from the author, except in the case of brief quotations embodied in articles or reviews.

Front cover photo credit: Depositphotos

Requests for such permission should be addressed to:

Priceless Parenting
11107 NE 174th Street
Bothell, WA 98011

425-770-1629

www.PricelessParenting.com

Table of Contents

Author's Introduction 7
Chapter 1: Guiding and Encouraging Children 9
    Envisioning Your Ideal Home 11
    Mindfully Parenting by Pausing and Planning 13
    Leading Your Kids Without Bossing Them 17
    Setting a Positive Tone 19
    Treating Each Other with Respect 21
    Giving Your Kids Appropriate Control 25
    Helping Children Solve Their Own Problems 29
    Giving Children Responsibilities 31
    Developing Children's Empathy and Compassion 33
    Focusing on Positive Behavior 38
    Nurturing Your Child's Soul, Not Just Their Mind and Body 40
    Encouraging Self-Motivation 44
    Setting Limits Around Media Usage 46
    Talking About the Birds and the Bees 48
    Protecting Your Kids from Sexual Abuse 50
    Making Time to be Together 52
Chapter 2: Parenting Behaviors to Avoid 55
    Avoiding Negative Techniques 57
    Seeking Revenge Through Punishment 58
    Hitting Children 59
    Yelling at Children 60
    Nagging and Ordering Children Around 61
    Doing Things for Children that They Can Do for Themselves 62
    Bribing Children 63
    Giving in To Keep Kids Happy 64
    Threatening or Scaring Children 65

Lecturing and Over Explaining ... 66
Battling Over Food ... 67
Arguing Over Homework ... 68
Saying "I told you so!" or "Because I said so!" ... 69
Reacting Before Understanding ... 70
Breaking Promises ... 71
Spending in Ways that Create Entitled Kids ... 72
Sneaking, Spying or Snooping ... 73
Shaming Publicly or Privately ... 74

Chapter 3: Responding Positively to Misbehavior ... 75
Choosing New Approaches ... 77
Challenging Behavior Worksheet ... 78
Asking Your Children for Ideas ... 79
Letting Children Solve Their Own Problems ... 80
Allowing Natural Consequences to Teach ... 81
Choosing Appropriate Consequences ... 82
Finding Solutions Instead of Issuing Consequences ... 83
Resolving Conflicts Using Collaborative & Proactive Solutions ... 84
Shaping the Desired Behaviors ... 86
Using Short Responses ... 89
Saying What You Will Do Instead of What They Have To Do ... 90
Asking Once ... 91
Turning a "No" into a "Yes" ... 92
Setting Effective Limits ... 93
Identifying Underlying Emotions ... 94
Standing Firm Without Arguing ... 95
Waiting for Compliance ... 96
Teaching Children to Use "I Statements" ... 97
Telling Children What They Can Do ... 98
Taking "Cool Down" Time ... 99
Establishing Simple Rules ... 100

Seeking Outside Help 101

Chapter 4: Building Your Kids' Life Skills 103

Expressing Emotions in Healthy Ways 105

Controlling Negative Thoughts 110

Helping Your Kids Overcome Fear and Anxiety 112

Setting Healthy Limits 115

Building Friendship Skills 117

Developing Habits to Succeed in School 122

Persevering Through Challenges 125

Learning through Chores 127

Teaching Financial Responsibility 130

Following Important Rules 132

Building Kids' Confidence Through Creativity 136

Chapter 5: Leading with Your Best Parenting 139

Striving To Do Your Best 141

Setting Healthy Boundaries Within Your Family 146

Understanding Men and Women React Differently to Stress 149

Pulling Together as a Family with Weekly Family Meetings 151

Identifying Your Family's Top 5 Moral Values 154

Responding to Kids with Compassion Instead of Criticism 159

Successfully Tackling Difficult Conversations 164

Positively Focusing Emotional Energy 168

Recognizing Red Flag Behaviors - Clues Kids Aren't Coping Well 171

Reducing Suicide Among Kids 175

Following Your Parenting Intuition 177

Habitually Responding in Helpful Ways to Parenting Situations 179

Conclusion 181

About the Author 183

Index 185

References and Notes 187

Author's Introduction

Welcome! Parenting is a long journey with many twists and turns. My hope is that this book will help you successfully navigate through it all.

Although kids don't come with manuals, there is a universal body of knowledge about how loving parents raise respectful, responsible children. This book will guide you through exploring parenting ideas and trying them out with your own children.

You will learn about parenting approaches that work well based on research and real family stories. When parents implement these best practices, they report having a lot more joy in their homes and a lot less yelling and nagging!

The first chapter focuses on key elements for guiding and encouraging your kids. The second chapter discusses parenting techniques to avoid – tempting though they may be! The third chapter provides alternative approaches in responding to kids' misbehavior. The fourth chapter dives into building the life skills your kids will need to successfully launch as young adults. The final chapter includes ideas for doing your best parenting.

Sharing important parenting ideas is my life's work. I founded Priceless Parenting in 2007 to help give all parents access to this critical information.

Priceless Parenting has transformed thousands of formerly frazzled families from across the United States to Australia. These families have become happier and more harmonious using what they've learned through online parenting classes, presentations and parent coaching.

Parenting can be a pleasure or a pain. When you have the right tools, you will experience more pleasure. The goal of this book is to give you those essential tools. Taking the time to develop your parenting skills is one of the best investments you can make for your family.

Please feel free to contact me if you have questions or would like to schedule a presentation or parent coaching session.

I wish you and your family all the best!

Kathy Slattengren

Kathy@PricelessParenting.com
425-770-1629

Chapter 1: Guiding and Encouraging Children

Priceless® Parenting

This chapter examines key elements for building a positive family life. Each section has questions to help you think through how you can apply these ideas to your family.

Envisioning Your Ideal Home

Parenting is the most difficult job most of us will ever have. It is also an incredibly important job – the way you handle parenting will greatly affect your future happiness. This book is designed to help you think through various parenting choices.

How you react to your children daily affects your relationship with them. By choosing approaches which involve being compassionate and providing guidance, you will build warm, loving relationships with your children. This chapter explores parenting behaviors that help build a strong foundation for understanding and guiding your children.

You can create the home of your dreams!

Begin by thinking back to when you were anticipating the arrival of your first child.

What were your dreams for this new family you were starting?

What type of home you did you hope to create?

I dreamed of creating a home that feels:

- **Welcoming**: Everyone in the family feels safe and secure. Home is a comfortable place to be and to share with friends.

- **Accepting**: Individuals are accepted for who they are and appreciated for their unique gifts, talents and contributions.

- **Supportive**: Family members help each other out.

- **Peaceful**: Disagreements and misbehavior are handled without yelling or hitting.

- **Positive**: The general tone of interactions between family members is constructive.

- **Encouraging**: When someone is struggling, others find ways to provide hope and encouragement.

Envisioning the type of home you want to create is the first step in making it a reality. Answer the questions on the next page to get started. Come back and update your answers as you think of new ideas.

What qualities would you like in your ideal home?

_____
_____
_____
_____
_____

Which of these qualities are currently missing from your home?

_____
_____
_____
_____
_____

What is one change you could make that would positively affect how your home feels?

_____
_____
_____
_____
_____

Mindfully Parenting by Pausing and Planning

How do you feel when your kids misbehave? If you're like most parents, when your kids misbehave you experience feelings of anger, frustration or discouragement.

When you act immediately in your negative emotional state, you are likely to come up with your worst parenting responses. You may find yourself doing things like:

- Yelling at your kids - "I'm never taking you here again!" (even though you probably will be going back to the grocery store at some point)

- Threatening them - "I'll just leave you here!" (even though it is not legal to abandon your kids at McDonalds)

- Saying things you soon regret and they don't forget - "You are a disgrace to our family!" (even though you don't mean it)

- Hitting them (even though you promised you'd never do that)

Reacting emotionally to children's behavior leads to poor parenting choices.

Ouch! Why are these types of responses so easy to fall into?

Responding with Fight-or-Flight

When you are upset with your kids, your body is triggered into a fight-or-flight response. The fight-or-flight response is a natural physical reaction to a perceived threat or harmful event. Chemicals flood your body in preparation for fighting or fleeing. Your heart beats faster, your blood pressure goes up, your breathing quickens plus many other things which your body does automatically.

At this point you are ready to fight or run away but you are in a poor position to make a wise parenting response. In her book, The Willpower Instinct: How Self-Control Works, Why It Matters, and What You Can Do To Get More of It, psychologist Kelly McGonigal explains "The fight-or-flight response floods the body with energy to act instinctively, and steals it from the areas of the brain needed for wise decision making."[1]

No wonder it's hard to think straight! Your ability to think clearly is temporarily hijacked when these chemicals get released. Your body is responding perfectly if you are about to be mugged or attacked by a dog. However, it's not the best response if you are dealing with your children's misbehavior.

Mindfully Responding with Pause-and-Plan

How can you overcome this fight-or-flight response and re-engage the thinking parts of your brain? You need to mindfully respond instead of just reacting. Dr. Justin Parent, researcher on mindfulness, has identified "three key factors to mindful parenting:

1. Noticing your own feelings when you're in conflict with your child,

2. Learning to pause before responding in anger,

3. Listening carefully to a child's viewpoint even when disagreeing with it."[2]

First you need to be aware of your feelings. Your feelings provide important information about how you are interpreting a situation. You then need to engage the pause-and-plan response.

McGonigal describes the way it works. "Your brain needs to bring the body on board with your goals and put the brakes on your impulses. To do this, your prefrontal cortex will communicate the need for self-control to lower brain regions that regulate your heart rate, blood pressure, breathing, and other automatic functions. The pause-and-plan response drives you in the opposite direction of the fight-or-flight response. Instead of speeding up, your heart slows down, and your blood pressure stays normal. Instead of hyperventilating like a madman, you take a deep breath. Instead of tensing muscles to prime them for action, your body relaxes a little."[3]

One of the easiest ways to do this is to focus on your breathing. If you can intentionally slow your breathing down to about six breaths per minute, you will cause your body to relax.

Once you pause and calm down, you will be in a better position to respond in a helpful way. Pausing allows you to consider the big picture instead of immediate, short-term goals.

Listening Carefully to Understand

The final step is listening to your child. Listening is one of those skills that really doesn't seem like it's all that difficult. Why then do so many children report that their parents don't listen to them?

Maybe it's because there are a lot of ways to unintentionally stop conversations with your kids. For example, pretend your child has asked you for permission to go to a friend's house. You've explained that it is too late in the evening given it is a school night. Your child is continuing to beg to go for just an hour. These types of responses will leave your child feeling unheard:

- **Criticizing**: "What's wrong with you? You know it's too late to go out now when you have school tomorrow."

- **Labeling**: "You are acting like a spoiled brat!"

- **Analyzing**: "You always try to test my patience. You think if you irritate me enough I'll give in. That is so not happening!"

- **Diverting:** "Do you have all your homework done?"

- **Reassuring**: "You can go over to your friend's house on Saturday. That's just two days from now."

- **Giving Advice**: "You should plan ahead a little better. If you had asked an hour ago it would have worked but now it is too late."

- **Lecturing**: "You can't always do what you want to do. You just saw each other at school today and you'll see each other tomorrow too. Sometimes you have to learn to wait."

These types of responses are considered roadblocks to conversation because they tend to shutdown communication. It is extremely easy to accidentally use these roadblocks when talking to your children.

If you want your children to feel heard, a better approach is to

- **Stop** what you are doing

- **Look** at your child

- **Listen** carefully - pay attention to the body language

- When your child is done speaking, **summarize** what you heard

When you summarize what you heard, you are giving your child the opportunity to clarify or correct your understanding. In the example of your child wanting to go to the friend's house you might say "You feel disappointed that I'm not allowing you to go." Your child may reply "I'm mad!". You adjust to your child's clarification saying, "You're mad I won't allow you to go."

Good listening takes time, patience and attention. You can't fully listen while also using your phone or working on a computer. Communication involves not only words but also body language, eye contact and tone of voice. So to understand your child's message, you need to both hear the words and watch how they are said.

Listening to your children while resisting the urge to jump in and solve the problem is not easy. You could solve the problem by allowing your child to go to the friend's house. However, that will teach your child that begging works and encourage more begging in the future. Instead you can hear your children's concerns without changing your decision.

It takes plenty of practice before mindful responses become second nature. With determination, you can make pause-and-plan your typical response to your children's behavior instead of fight-or-flight.

Practice mindfully responding with pause-and-plan. Describe three situations where you used a mindful response with your children.

1. _____

_____

_____

2. _____

_____

_____

3. _____

_____

_____

Leading Your Kids Without Bossing Them

Do you liked to be bossed around? Probably not! How does the thought of being managed by someone else make you feel? Irritated? Angry? Rebellious? If you're like most, you react negatively to someone trying to boss or control you.

Your children are no different. They also do not like when you try to control their behavior. You can test this out by watching their reaction to commands like "Hurry up!", "Stop fighting!" or "Quit your whining."

Your role as a parent is similar to being a boss, manager or leader. If you shy away from being the boss in your family and try instead to be your children's friend, that leaves your family without the strong leadership it really needs.

Considering the Characteristics of Your Favorite Boss

Think about your favorite boss or manager. What qualities made this person such a good boss?

These are some of the important characteristics listed by parents:

- Empathetic
- Honest
- Generous
- Enthusiastic
- Consistent
- Fun, sense of humor
- Positive attitude
- Inspirational
- Compassionate
- Trustworthy
- Fully present

Your children will respond better to being led than to being bossed.

The qualities of an excellent boss apply equally to parents. By developing these traits, you will be an admired leader in your family.

Becoming an Admired Leader Instead of a Despised Boss

If you're a parent with children at home, then you are the leader. It's up to you to oversee providing for the family, making the major decisions and setting firm limits for your children. Families become dysfunctional when parents abandon their leadership role.

David explained in exasperation about how his 13-year-old son does "whatever he damn well pleases". He sadly described that he knew his son need stronger boundaries but was at a loss as to how effectively to influence his son's behavior.

For example, his son came home two hours late one night. Although he yelled at his son, the next day his son was late again. While yelling in anger is a natural response, it doesn't match the characteristics of excellent leadership. What else could David have done?

He could have approached his son with honesty and empathy while also working towards a consistent solution. David might have explained, "I was really worried when you didn't come home on time. I understand you were having fun and lost track of the time. How do you think we can change things so this doesn't happen again?" Involving his son in figuring out the solution will increase the likelihood of his son sticking to their agreement.

Developing Your Leadership Qualities

Developing leadership qualities is a lifelong process. Think about the characteristics of your favorite leaders and decide which one you would most like to work on. The more you develop your leadership skills, the better leader you will be for your family.

Which leadership qualities do you feel are most important for you to have?

_____

_____

_____

Setting a Positive Tone

Parents play a lead role in setting the overall tone in their families. Parents whose overall tone tends to be negative often have homes filled with stress and tension. On the other hand, parents who use a more positive approach create calmer, happier homes.

Sometimes parents get in the habit of interacting with their children using negative statements and commands. Read the following statements one dad made to his children and think about how you would feel if you were a child hearing these remarks:

- "You aren't going outside until you put sunscreen on."
- "Stop messing around with that!"
- "If you don't hurry up and get your shoes on, I'm not taking you."
- "You've already watched too much TV. You should not have turned it on again, now turn it off."
- "You're not eating dinner until you wash your hands."
- "You are dawdling and we're going to be late!"
- "Stop bugging your sister!"

The words you choose create the tone they hear.

How do you feel after reading these statements? Let's look at how these same ideas could be expressed more positively:

- "Feel free to go outside as soon as you put sunscreen on."
- "That could break so you can play with this instead."
- "I am leaving in two minutes. I'll be happy to take you if have your shoes on."
- "Your TV time is up for today. Would you like to turn the TV off or would you like me to turn it off?"
- "Please wash your hands and then join us for dinner."
- "We're leaving in 5 minutes. Do you plan to be dressed or will you be taking your clothes in a bag?"

- "Your sister wants to be left alone right now. Do you want to play a game with me or go outside?"

How do you feel now? The words you use make a huge difference! Using more positive statements demonstrates an unspoken belief that your children are capable and are likely to choose appropriate behavior.

For the next few days, try paying attention to what you say to your children. If you hear yourself say something negative, figure out how you might communicate the same thing more positively. Here's some other questions to consider:

How did you greet your children first thing this morning?

___

___

___

When your children misbehave, what is your normal reaction?

___

___

___

When your children return home from school, what do you usually say to them?

___

___

___

Treating Each Other with Respect

Treating each other with respect is a fundamental quality of healthy relationships. When your children treat you with respect, they honor your worth and dignity. Likewise, when you treat your children with respect, you honor their worth and dignity.

Both you and your kids want to feel valued and have your needs taken into consideration. When this happens, everyone feels respected.

Respectful Versus Disrespectful Behavior

What does respect look like to you? When your children are treating you with respect, what are they doing?

Showing respect is key to healthy relationships.

Here are some ways your children may be showing respect:

- Listening to you
- Saying please and thank you
- Waiting a turn to talk without interrupting
- Helping with household tasks
- Telling you where they are going and when they'll be back
- Calling or texting if they will be home late

What do your kids do that you consider disrespectful? How do you feel when your kids are being disrespectful? Disrespectful behavior tends to trigger strong emotions so it quickly catches your attention.

Some disrespectful behavior you may see from your kids include:

- Talking back
- Ignoring you
- Hitting you
- Refusing reasonable requests
- Rolling their eyes at you

Nobody likes being treated disrespectfully! You cannot force your children to treat you with respect. However, how you respond to disrespectful behavior makes a big difference in how your kids behave in the future.

Setting Boundaries on Disrespectful Behavior

A boundary establishes the line between behaviors that are OK and those that are not. Disrespectful behavior from your kids crosses the boundary into behavior that is not OK.

Have you ever seen a young child hit their parent while the parent ignores what is happening? Ignoring disrespectful behavior sends the unspoken message is that it is fine to act that way.

What if your child hit you? How could you set a boundary? One way is to take your child's hands in yours, look straight in her eyes declaring "It is not OK to hit me. Our rule is you hit, you sit. So you need to sit right here for three minutes."

When your kids are acting disrespectfully, there are often big feelings behind their behavior. Their feelings are not right or wrong. The way they choose to express their feelings crosses the boundary if it is disrespectful.

You can always acknowledge their feelings while setting a limit on their behavior. Suppose your child is angry and says "You're so unfair! I hate you!" You might respond "I know you're angry. You need to find other words to tell me about your anger."

How do you handle your child being disrespectful in a public situation? You can choose to delay fully dealing with the disrespectful behavior. You might say "That is not OK. We'll talk about it when we get home." When you do get home be sure to follow up on it.

Showing Respect by Expressing Gratitude

You are responsible for teaching your children to say "please" and "thank you". This basic social skill is critical in showing respect for others.

It takes plenty of prompting and teaching when kids are young. It's worth the effort because developing the skill of showing appreciation will benefit your kids as they get older. It's essential in maintaining relationships.

Considering other people's feelings can be challenging for kids. Part of showing genuine appreciation involves being able to put yourself in someone else's shoes. When children haven't fully developed this skill, it can cause problems.

For example, one aunt explained how hard she worked to find neat gifts for her three nephews. When opening the gifts, they would often say things like "I don't really like this." or "This isn't what I wanted." The aunt felt hurt by these remarks. Unfortunately, the parents did not step in to help their sons learn that these types of responses were inappropriate and unkind.

At another holiday gathering children were wildly opening gifts without paying much attention to who the gift was from never mind thanking the person for the gift. The children threw aside each gift and anxiously started tearing the wrapping from the next gift. Again, the parents failed to set up appropriate rules or expectations for the gift opening.

Teaching How To Show Appreciation

It's critical to teach your children how to politely handle situations involving gifts. It can be helpful to sit down with your kids ahead of time and discuss the importance of showing their thankfulness. Discussing and practicing what to say under various situations can help prepare your kids to act graciously.

What might you tell your kids to do in the situation where they receive a gift they really aren't excited about? If the gift giver is right there, it could be a simple thank you with a hug. If the gift giver is not nearby, your child could call or write a thank you. Your child can always thank the person for their thoughtfulness in giving the gift.

What if your kids forget to say thank you? It is helpful to agree on a gentle reminder signal ahead of time. For example, you might lightly touch your child on the ear as a reminder.

Avoid expressing appreciation on behalf of your children instead of guiding them to saying thank you. When you show appreciation instead of your kids, they do not learn that it is their responsibility to say thank you for things they've received. Children who do not learn to show these basic courtesies are often disrespectful in several other ways.

Chapter 1: Guiding and Encouraging Children   © Priceless Parenting

Birthdays and holidays provide many opportunities for children to practice expressing their appreciation. Be sure to give your children the gift of learning to express their gratitude!

If your children forget to say thank you, how would they like you to remind them?

_____

_____

_____

How have you demonstrated treating your children with respect?

_____

_____

_____

How have you set boundaries when your children were disrespectful?

_____

_____

_____

Giving Your Kids Appropriate Control

Everyone likes control over their lives. You encourage power struggles when you try to control something that your children ultimately control. In her book, <u>Positive Discipline</u>, Jane Nelsen explains "Excessive control invites rebellion or resistance, instead of encouraging children to learn the skills these parents want to teach." [4]

Trying to Control Using Commands

Moments of frustration can lead you to issuing commands to try to control your children's behavior. Any time you are ordering your children to change their behavior you are not likely to succeed. Instead of producing the desired behavioral change, commands often lead to some type of resistance.

For example, when feeling stressed to leave on time, you may yell to your children "Hurry up! It's time to get going!" It can feel good to give commands because it seems like you have more control over a situation when you're shouting commands. However, children often resist being told what to do (interestingly, most adults also do not like being told what to do)!

When children are given appropriate control, they have little need to rebel.

Since children ultimately control their own behavior, commands like these are usually ineffective:

- "Stop crying!"
- "No more whining."
- "Don't give me that look."
- "Go to sleep right now!"

It is easy to fall into the parenting trap of using commands to try and control kids' behavior. However, it is far more effective to tell children what you are going to do instead of what they must do. You might declare "I'm leaving in five minutes." instead of saying "Hurry up!"

Telling Them What You Are Going To Do

A dad was trying to change his 18-month-old daughter's diaper while she was crying and struggling to get away. When doing an unappealing task like changing a diaper, it's difficult to have a child who is resisting and making an unpleasant task even more unpleasant.

This dad responded by telling his daughter "Stop crying!" Not only did she not stop crying, her crying intensified. It was easy to relate to his frustration as well as his child's reaction.

In this case, the dad probably would have been more successful by empathizing with his daughter by saying something like "I can see you're really upset. I'm going to change your diaper and then we will leave." By acknowledging her feelings and telling her what he was going to do, he could avoid telling her what she had to do.

Sometimes in the heat of the moment, you may not do your best parenting. Later, it can be helpful to reflect on how you wish you would have handled the situation. You are likely to have a second chance soon to handle a similar situation in a better way!

Considering Who Controls What

Power struggles are likely to be ignited when you try to control your kids' behavior. Below are some examples of things children and parents' control.

Child Controls	Parent Controls
the food they choose to eat	the food that is purchased
when they go to sleep	when they are in their bedrooms
their tone of voice	how you respond to that tone of voice
how hard they work at school	whether they go to school
whether they use the bathroom	whether they are given the opportunity to use the bathroom
their behavior	your behavior

When you feel like you are in a power struggle, step back and think. Are you trying to control something that they really control? Is there some way you could give them more control in the situation?

Sharing Control Through Choices

Everyone loves choices including kids! Choices are a wonderful way to give children control and help them learn from making decisions.

When you give your children choices, you are sharing control within limits. For example, you may give your kids the choice of milk, juice or water to drink. You set the limits by choosing the available options. If your child says they want pop, you can calmly repeat their choices.

You want to ensure your children have solid decision-making skills before they are teens. This is critical because as teens they will start making serious decisions when you are not around.

By giving children lots of choices when they are young, they'll be practicing making decisions and anticipating the consequences of those decisions. Your job as a parent is so much easier when your children make wise decisions on their own.

"Life is the sum of all your choices."
~Albert Camus

Giving Choices Reduces Rebellion

When parents try to control their children's behavior, the result is often children who rebel. Rebelling is a way to resist their parents attempt to control them.

In her book Wonderful Ways to Love a Child, Judy Ford states "A child who trusts you to respect his independence has little need to rebel. The most rebellious and depressed adults are those who, as children, were the most strictly controlled. They were not allowed to find their own identity or make their own choices. Right or wrong, they were forced to dutifully follow their parent's authority."[5]

Cooperation Increases with Choices

Giving young children choices can make them more cooperative. One mom was battling with her son over using the bathroom. One day instead of telling him to go use the bathroom she asked him "Do you want to gallop or walk to the bathroom?" She was surprised that he galloped to the bathroom without arguing!

Older children are also more agreeable when they have input into decisions that matter to them. For example, if teens get to choose their household chores, they're more likely to get their chores done with minimal grumbling!

By the time teens are graduating from high school, they will need to make important choices about what to do next in their lives. The more practice they've had making choices all along, the more capable they will be of thinking through critical decisions.

Here are some examples of turning commands into choices:

Commands	Choices
Go take your bath.	Do you want to take a bath upstairs or downstairs?
Do your homework.	Would you like to do your homework before dinner or after dinner?
Get dressed.	Would you prefer to get dressed at home or at preschool?
Go practice the piano.	You are welcome to practice the piano with the door shut or the door open.
Brush your teeth.	You can either brush your teeth or ask me to help you brush them.

Try giving your kids lots of choices and write down some of the choices you gave them.

_____

_____

_____

_____

How did your children handle these choices? What do you think they learned?

_____

_____

_____

_____

Helping Children Solve Their Own Problems

When your children come to you with a problem, it can be tempting to just solve the problem for them. However, if you want them to learn to solve similar problems in the future, it is better to guide them through finding a solution.

In her book, Easy to Love, Difficult to Discipline, Dr. Becky Bailey describes a process to help children solve their own problems[6]. She uses the acronym **PEACE** to make the steps easier to remember:

1. Discern who owns the **p**roblem.

2. Offer **e**mpathy to the child.

3. **A**sk the child to think, "What do you think you are going to do?"

4. Offer **c**hoices and suggestions.

5. **E**ncourage the child to come up with his own solution.

Remember to begin by connecting with empathy before working towards a solution.

Let's look at an example of using this process. Suppose 4-year-old Ben runs to you crying because his 2-year-old sister Anna has knocked down his block structure. Here's how the PEACE process might go:

1. You realize this is Ben's problem.

2. You show empathy by hugging Ben and saying "I can see you're really sad. You worked hard on building that."

3. You ask Ben "What do you think you are going to do?"

4. Ben comes up with one idea; he wants to hit his sister. You quickly ask what is likely to happen if he does that! He decides not to do this but doesn't know what else to do. You offer the idea that he could build with the blocks in his room with the door shut. Ben rejects this idea because he wants to build in the living room. You suggest he could build when Anna is napping. Ben also rejects this idea.

5. You say, "I'm sure you'll find a good solution." You've given him a couple ideas and you are leaving him with the responsibility for coming up with his own solution.

Here's one more example of using this process. This time let's pretend your 10-year-old daughter comes to you upset because she's forgotten her math assignment at school and it is due tomorrow. Here's how you might handle it:

1. You remember this is your daughter's problem since it's her homework.

2. Show empathy: "I can understand why you are upset."

3. Ask her "What do you think you are going to do?"

4. She's thought about going back to school to get it, but she knows the teacher is already gone and the classroom door is locked. She doesn't know what else to do. You suggest calling a classmate to see if she can get a copy of the homework. When you ask her how this might work out, she replies that she's going to try giving Sara a call.

5. You reply "Great! I hope she can give you a copy of the homework or read off the problems to you." You leave it up to her to call Sara and resolve the problem.

Once again you are guiding your child through the problem without providing the solution or insisting on what she should do.

Use the PEACE process to guide your child through a problem. Write down what happened along with anything you might do differently in the future.

_____

_____

_____

_____

_____

Giving Children Responsibilities

As children grow older, they are continually ready for new responsibilities (although they probably won't be asking for these new responsibilities)! From getting dressed to preparing a meal, kids need increasing responsibilities to grow into competent adults.

Children are often capable of more responsibility than they are given. When you take on responsibilities which your children really should be handling, you are likely to feel overwhelmed and underappreciated.

Giving your children responsibilities increases their competence.

One mom complained about all the extra work she was doing now that her 3rd and 6th graders were back in school. In just one day, she did all these extra tasks after they finished school:

- Tried to pick her daughter up early from school for a piano lesson. Her daughter forgot and took the bus home. Lectured her on the importance of remembering her piano lessons.

- Dumped out the kids' backpacks and sorted through papers.

- Worked on making dinner while being interrupted numerous times to help with homework.

- Ran to the store to buy purple shirts after the kids announced that they needed to wear purple tomorrow for Spirit Day.

- Packed forms and supplies into each child's backpack.

- Spent 10 minutes looking for library books due the next day.

- Packed lunches for the next day.

- Did a load of laundry after one child reported having no clean socks.

- Yelled at the kids to GO TO BED NOW!

- Got her youngest a drink of water.

Mom then collapsed into bed. Anyone would be exhausted after a day like that!

It is easy for parents to take on responsibilities that their children could handle. What tasks do you think this mom could let her kids handle?

The girls are probably old enough to take responsibility for sorting through their school papers, finding their library books, packing their lunches, preparing their backpacks for the next day, doing laundry and getting a drink of water.

Which tasks could be skipped? While the girls will be disappointed if they don't have purple shirts for Spirit Day, they may be inspired to plan better in the future. Although clean socks are nice, wearing a dirty pair of socks one day will not actually kill a child!

Which items could be reduced with limits or consequences? Lecturing her daughter about missing her piano lesson does little to help her daughter remember in the future. If her daughter had to pay for the missed lesson or write an apology note to her teacher, she's more likely to remember the lesson in the future.

Dinner preparation could be less stressful by limiting homework help to other times. For example, she could establish homework help time between 3:00 – 4:00 and 7:00 – 8:00.

When you take on responsibilities your children really could be handling or fail to set limits, you are likely to feel overwhelmed.

What tasks are you doing for your children that they could be doing?

_____

_____

_____

What is one new responsibility your child is ready to take on?

_____

_____

_____

Developing Children's Empathy and Compassion

Children are not born with empathy. They are born with the capacity to have empathy, but it only develops under certain conditions. You play a critical role in developing your children's empathy.

In their book, <u>Born for Love: Why Empathy is Essential - and Endangered</u>, Perry and Szalavitz write "The essence of empathy is the ability to stand in another's shoes, to feel what it's like there and to care about making it better if it hurts."[7] They document numerous cases where children have not experienced adequate empathy while growing up. These kids' behavior towards others also reflects a lack of empathy which can lead to serious problems.

"The great gift of human beings is that we have the power of empathy."
~ Meryl Streep

Three key things you can do to develop your children's empathy are:

Key 1: Show empathy when responding to their behavior.

Children learn to be empathetic by being treated with empathy. This begins when they are babies with loving adults responding to their cries and needs. Soothing young children when they are upset lays the foundation for their own development of empathy.

Older children learn empathy when you respond to their behavior in a caring way rather than with anger. Instead of yelling "How could you do that?" or "What were you thinking?" respond in a way that demonstrates you understand what your child is going through. For example, if your child spilled juice, you might say "Oops! That's unfortunate. Let me know if you need any help cleaning it up."

Reflecting your child's feelings is another way of showing empathy. If your child has angrily thrown her math book, you could say "I can see you're frustrated. I get frustrated too when I'm having trouble doing something." Empathy puts you and your child on the same side of the problem.

Key 2: Demonstrate genuine empathy.

When using empathy, it needs to come from your heart. If it doesn't sound genuine, children will quickly see through it as fake empathy.

One mom of two teens complained that she tried to be empathetic to their problems but it only seemed to make them mad. She went on to explain that she would often respond to their problems by saying "bummer". Instead of feeling genuinely understood, they felt angry because it seemed like she was belittling them.

To see a situation from your child's viewpoint, it can help to think of a situation where you've experienced something similar to what your child is experiencing. For example, if you've ever ordered a meal at a restaurant and then regretted your choice when the meal came, you can understand how your child might feel in a similar situation like the following one.

Pretend you asked your child, "What would you like for breakfast: cereal, pancakes or toast?" Suppose your child chooses cereal but when you place the cereal in front of her she says "I changed my mind. I want pancakes." You may be tempted to yell "You asked for cereal; I got you cereal; Now eat it!"

Instead you could show understanding by responding with something like "Now that you have your cereal you're disappointed you didn't choose pancakes. Tomorrow morning you can choose pancakes." If she becomes upset, it's better to acknowledge her feelings again with something like "I realize you are upset. Tomorrow you can have pancakes." instead of "Stop complaining and eat!"

Key 3: Discuss other people's perspectives

Reading books can help develop understanding of others' viewpoints. Ask your kids why they think characters are acting in a certain way. How are those characters feeling? What are they thinking?

You can have this same type of discussion with the events happening in your children's lives. For example, if a new student has joined your child's class, you can talk to your child about how it must feel to be a new student in the class and to not know anyone yet. By trying to understand how this new student is feeling, your child may be inspired to find ways to help this new student feel more comfortable.

When you help your children see the world from different viewpoints you help them develop their empathy. When children can feel empathy for others, they are far less likely to engage in behaviors like bullying.

Encouraging Kids To Act With Compassion

Before your children can act compassionately, they need to be able to feel empathy for others. Without empathy there is no compassion.

Children must first notice that someone is suffering before they can act in a helpful way.

When your children feel empathy, they can imagine what it must be like for that other person. Children often want to do something to help. Compassion requires acting on empathic feelings and doing something to lessen the other person's suffering.

Feeling empathy without acting to help can lead to feelings of distress. In Daniel Goleman's book, <u>A Force For Good: The Dalai Lama's Vision for Our World</u>, he explains, "When we simply empathize, tuning in to someone else's suffering – for example, seeing vivid photos of burn victims and other people in grave distress – the brain fires the circuitry for feeling pain and anguish. Such empathic resonance can flood us with emotional upset – 'empathy distress', as science calls it. Professionals like nursing are too often plagued by such chronic anxiety, which can build to emotional exhaustion, a precursor to burnout."[8]

Goleman continues "Compassion, the findings suggest, serves as an inoculation against empathy distress, with more activity in the brain centers for caring, which builds resiliency instead of burnout." Guiding your children to turning their empathy into action helps both them and others.

Showing Empathy Versus Showing Compassion

Compassion involves putting your time, energy and resources where your heart is. Compassion requires the courage to act when it's easier not to.

For example, if your child sees another child sitting alone at lunch and feels bad for that child that's empathy. If your child chooses to sit down with that student for lunch that's showing compassion.

If your child watches somebody being bullied and feels bad for them that's empathy. If your child sees somebody being bullied and stands next to them to provide support that's compassion.

Children have a great capacity for empathy and compassion. They may need your help in implementing their ideas. For example, some children in the Seattle area heard about wildfires that had burned several homes in Eastern Washington. They decided to have a bake sale to raise money to help the people who lost their homes. Their parents helped them organize it and donate the money.

Guiding Children Towards Compassion

Being able to put themselves in someone else's shoes is a skill that develops as children mature. Sometimes kids benefit from having someone else help them see things from another's perspective.

In his book The Boy Who Was Raised as a Dog, Dr. Bruce Perry describes Peter, a first-grade boy whose parents adopted him from Russia. Peter spent his first three years of his life in an orphanage primarily stuck in a crib. His parents were seeking help from Dr. Perry due to a number of Peter's behavioral issues. Because he didn't get the loving interactions he needed early on, his social skills were far behind other children his age.

Dr. Perry realized that Peter's peers were in the best position to help him learn these social skills so he spoke to Peter's first grade class. He explained why Peter's brain was different than theirs and how they could help Peter. Afterwards he writes "The brightest and strongest children in his class took a special interest in him and their leadership made all the difference. They included him, protected him and, ultimately, provided therapeutic experiences that helped Peter catch up. They were tolerant of his developmental problems, patient in correcting his social mistakes and nurturing in their interactions."[9]

Before Dr. Perry's visit, the children avoided Peter. After Dr. Perry helped Peter's classmates replace fear of Peter with empathy, the children acted with compassion.

You can encourage compassion in your kids by asking questions like "What did you do today to help someone?" When you ask about something every day, your kids get the message that this is important to you. Your positive attention to your children's stories will reinforce their kind behavior.

Benefitting from Compassion

When children show compassion, they also benefit. In A Force For Good: The Dalai Lama's Vision for Our World, Goleman reports "In research at the University of North Carolina, practicing an attitude of loving-kindness not only lessened depression and boosted positive moods but also increased sense of satisfaction with their lives, strengthening their connection with family and friends. ... Early findings on cultivating an attitude of compassion suggest even biological benefits, such as lessened inflammation and lowered levels of stress hormones."[10]

The scientific research supports these words from the Dalai Lama. "The human capacity to care for others isn't something trivial or something to be taken for granted. Rather, it is something we should cherish. Compassion is a marvel of human nature, a precious inner resource, and the foundation of our well-being and the harmony of our societies. If we seek happiness for ourselves, we should practice compassion: and if we seek happiness for others, we should also practice compassion."[11]

What ideas do your kids have for living more compassionately? When they act in ways that are motivated by genuine concern for others they are a force for good!

Practice responding to your children with empathy. What did you do?

_____

_____

_____

_____

What are some ways you can encourage your kids to act with compassion?

_____

_____

_____

_____

Focusing on Positive Behavior

Since you tend to get more of whatever you focus on, you definitely want to focus on your children's positive behavior! Simply paying attention to children when they are behaving well will increase the likelihood that they'll repeat that behavior.

Some parents accidentally provide plenty of attention only when their children are misbehaving. These children quickly learn that when they are throwing food on the floor or slamming doors, they will get their parent's attention. Children will repeat behaviors that get them attention even if it is negative attention.

You get more of whatever you focus on.

Commenting specifically on what you like is a way to give positive attention:

- "It was kind of you to share the truck with John."
- "Thank you for unloading the dishwasher."
- "I'm impressed with how quickly you got dressed."
- "I appreciate your help in putting the napkins on the table."

Your kids are more likely to repeat behavior that you've given them positive feedback on.

Describing What You See

How can you find something encouraging to say when your children are primarily misbehaving? Describe whatever you see that is not misbehavior. Remember that any attention is going to make your child feel noticed.

For example, perhaps your child has been using inappropriate language lately and you've noticed that the past half hour he hasn't sworn. You could say "I've noticed that you haven't sworn at all in the last 30 minutes. I appreciate that."

If your kids are often fighting with each other, look for an opportunity to comment when they are getting along. You might describe what they are doing. "You are playing together with the train tracks. You've worked to create a loop with three bridges along the way." Giving them attention when they are cooperating will encourage this behavior.

Perhaps your child struggles with math homework. You might comment "I see you handling your frustration as best you can. The math is hard and you're hanging in there and trying."

Ignoring Irritating Behavior

Likewise, ignoring negative behavior can help reduce it. If a behavior is irritating but not dangerous or cruel, try ignoring it.

For example, parents who ignore their children's fighting may be pleasantly surprised to see a reduction in sibling rivalry. Parents who attempt to intervene and stop the fighting often get the opposite results.

When you ignore your children's negative behavior and focus on their good behavior, you help them recognize their positive attributes.

What negative behavior might you decide to ignore?

_____

_____

_____

_____

Give some examples of how you've focused on your children's positive behavior.

_____

_____

_____

_____

Nurturing Your Child's Soul, Not Just Their Mind and Body

Raising a child is a huge commitment. You are responsible for nurturing not only your child's mind and body but also their soul. You receive help in nurturing your child's body right from the beginning. Nurses, midwives and pediatricians provide guidance on feeding and caring for your baby.

Soon you have help from various schools and organizations in developing your child's mind. Teachers, administrators and government officials all play a role. They influence what your children will learn at different ages.

Being a parent is a sacred responsibility. You have the power to crush your child's soul or help it to soar.

Where do you turn for help in nurturing your child's soul? If you belong to a religious community, you will receive direction from them. If you are not part of a religious community or want more support, where can you find it?

Finding Ways To Nurture Your Child's Soul

What does your child's soul need? One fundamental need is for your children to be seen and heard from their deepest selves.

How can you help your child feel seen and heard? Some things you can do include:

- Giving them your undivided attention for at least a few minutes every day

- Encouraging them to have their own opinions and ideas even if they don't match yours

- Showing respect for their bodies

- Treating them with kindness

- Allowing them to grow and change without trying to hold them back

- Seeking forgiveness and providing forgiveness

When you hold space for your children to share their thoughts and feelings, they deepen their understanding of their authentic selves. It's like you are holding a mirror up so that they can see their inner beauty.

Nurturing your children's souls involves encouraging them to develop a strong moral ground from which to use their gifts and talents. This includes things like:

- Having the courage to do what is right even when it's difficult
- Treating others with respect
- Showing compassion to others
- Being kind to all living creatures
- Taking care of the environment

When your children follow their values and morals, they will be able to best use their talents.

Providing Love and Approval

You nurture your child's soul when you provide love and approval. They need to feel like they belong in your family and are appreciated for who they are. When you let them know how much they mean to you, they are more likely to feel loved and act in positive ways.

Children pay great attention to what their parents focus on. If they hear a lot of praise for their accomplishments but not a lot of appreciation for being themselves, they may conclude that it's their achievements that matter most.

You can unintentionally reinforce this thinking by focusing on things like:

- Grades instead of effort
- Winning instead of playing the game fairly and to the best of their ability
- Being the top performer instead of achieving a personal best
- Doing something perfectly instead of doing as well as possible

One mom said that her 25-year-old daughter confessed that growing up she always tried to hide her struggles and failures from her mom. She felt her mom wanted her to be perfect and didn't want to disappoint her. This mom had never intended to give her daughter this message and was very surprised to learn that she felt this way.

What you notice about your children and how you say it matters. When you make comments about their character, they are more likely to realize it's who they are not what they do that matters most.

These types of comments reinforce positive character traits:

- "You were really generous to share that with your sister."
- "You are great at cheering your teammates on!"
- "Your smile always brightens up my day."
- "I am impressed with how hard you worked on that paper."

Another important way of demonstrating love is to hug your kids and say, "I love you." Some parents find this easier to do than others. It gets more challenging as children become teens and aren't the cuddly toddlers they once were. It's still important though even if they act like it's not!

Putting The Soul in Control

Developing self-control is essential for your children to live from their souls. Without self-control your child's body or mind will gladly fill in as the commander.

Allowing the mind or body to run the show can lead to problems like:

- Causing damage by acting out of anger
- Bullying, being mean to others
- Alcohol and drug addiction
- Internet and porn addiction
- Eating disorders

Your children are responsible for putting the brakes on their behavior. You can help your children stop poor behavior choices when they are young. However, the older they get the more they are responsible for making wise choices. Along with this increasing responsibility are increasing consequences from people outside your family.

Encouraging a Meaningful, Soul-Directed Life

As your kids grow up ideally they discover what they find most meaningful in life. It could be bringing others joy through playing music, cooking delicious meals, listening to problems, inventing ways to make life better or taking care of others. The possibilities are endless.

How do you help your children live authentically? Annie Burnside compares being a butterfly mom to a tiger mom in her book, From Role to Soul. In this excerpt she explains the desires she has for her children as a butterfly mom:

"Is success primarily about status, financial gain, and intellectual achievement stemming from a 'survival of the fittest' paradigm? As a butterfly mom, I hold a much different view of success. From a butterfly mom's perspective, success is much more about a child's metamorphosis from a beautiful, divine caterpillar – perfect already in every way despite any outward appearances to the contrary – into a conscious global citizen who knows their own heart. … the butterfly mom's deepest desire for her children is the ability to live true, courageously, and comfortably within their own skins. … Such children radiate a love of self and others. Fostering authenticity, which involves being liberated to live one's soul purpose, is the ultimate gift a butterfly mom offers her child."[12]

What is the ultimate gift you want to give your children? Instilling the courage to live their lives driven from their souls is a pretty special gift.

What characteristics do you admire in each of your children?

_____

_____

_____

_____

Encouraging Self-Motivation

How can you motivate your children to work harder in school, in a sport or in practicing an instrument? Will the promise of a reward for practicing the piano help your child practice more? Or will the threat of punishment be more effective? When you try to motivate your children to work harder, you can often end up feeling frustrated by the results.

Understanding Internal Motivation

Ideas about motivation are changing as new research teases out some of the key elements. According to Daniel Pink's book, <u>Drive: The Surprising Truth About What Motivates Us</u>, trying to motivate children using external rewards and punishment is a mistake.[13] The secret for motivating children to high performance lies in allowing their own internal drives to direct their behavior.

Pink describes three elements of true motivation:

- **Autonomy** - the need to direct our own lives

- **Mastery** - the desire to make progress in one's work

- **Purpose** - the ability to positively impact ourselves and our world

"Nothing great was ever achieved without enthusiasm."
~ *Ralph Waldo Emerson*

For example, if you want your child to practice the piano more, try allowing her to choose when to practice, what music to focus on and where to perform that will bring delight to someone else.

Trying to Control Too Much

When you try to motivate your children, it sometimes backfires as they dig in their heels and refuse to buckle under the pressure. By attempting to exert control over your children's behavior, you are reducing their autonomy - one of the key elements of internal motivation.

One mom was describing her frustration in getting her daughter to practice the piano. No matter how hard she tried her daughter sat on the piano bench refusing to put her fingers on the keys. This is a typical control battle and one that mom is likely to lose since her daughter ultimately controls what she does with her fingers!

How do you know when you've stepped over the line and are trying to control too much of your children's behavior? Luckily children are pretty good at letting you know when you've stepped over that line. If you hear your child saying the following, you're probably over the line:

- "You're not the boss of me!"
- "I'm not going to do that!"
- "You can't make me."
- "Why do you always get to choose?"

At this point it is wise to step back and look at what you are trying to accomplish. Consider other approaches that may yield better results.

Motivating to Perfection

Psychologist Robert W. Hill of Appalachian State University found that when people are trying hard because of their own desire for excellence, this effort can lead to greater satisfaction and mental health. However, if the pressure to perform is coming from others, it's likely to lead to dissatisfaction and reduced well-being.

In the article "The Two Faces of Perfection", Hill says "Kids need to get the message, 'You need to have high standards, but you don't need to be perfect.' If you have unreachable goals and you're constantly dissatisfied with yourself, you can be miserable. Unequivocally, you don't want a parent who is constantly criticizing, so the child develops a self-scrutiny that always finds fault with their own performance."[14]

While you want your children to try hard and make good choices, to accomplish this, you need to allow them to practice making those choices. They will make some poor choices and that will give them an opportunity to learn from their mistakes.

By giving your children the chance to develop their self-motivation, you encourage them to grow and find their own internal strengths.

When are your kids the most motivated? What do they gladly do without being asked?

_____

_____

Setting Limits Around Media Usage

When parents discuss how much media they allow their children, the answers vary wildly. Some parents have very strict time restrictions on their children's media viewing while others give their children more control over the time they spend on media.

How do you know when your child is getting too much media?

One mom knew she needed to allow less video game time when her 7-year-old son started not wanting play outside or do things with the family preferring his video game instead. He was so attached to playing his video game that he often pitched a fit when he was told the game had to go off. His games didn't have a good way to save the game for later so he was reluctant to stop playing and lose his place in the game.

Is over use of media negatively affecting your family's connection to each other?

She decided to reduce his video game playing to one hour twice a week. She started giving him a 10-minute warning before his hour was up. When the 10 minutes were up, he could either choose to shut the game off or she would turn the power off. It only took a couple times of turning the power off to get him to shut the game down in time.

What are signs that digital usage is becoming a problem?

If your children are exhibiting these types of behaviors, it's time to think about reducing the time they spend on media:

- Difficulty focusing on the present moment due to craving their video games or their cellphone

- Developing health issues such as Carpal Tunnel Syndrome, eye strain, weight gain, backaches

- Withdrawing from sports, hobbies and social interactions

- Losing sleep due to gaming, texting, being online

- Acting irritable or discontent when not using digital items

- Declining grades in school, missing school

- Talking and thinking obsessively about the digital activity

- Denying or minimizing any negative consequences

What do the experts recommend?

The American Academy of Pediatrics (AAP) recommends:

- "For children younger than 18 months, avoid use of screen media other than video-chatting. Parents of children 18 to 24 months of age who want to introduce digital media should choose high-quality programming, and watch it with their children to help them understand what they're seeing.

- For children ages 2 to 5 years, limit screen use to 1 hour per day of high-quality programs. Parents should co-view media with children to help them understand what they are seeing and apply it to the world around them.

- For children ages 6 and older, place consistent limits on the time spent using media, and the types of media, and make sure media does not take the place of adequate sleep, physical activity and other behaviors essential to health.

- Designate media-free times together, such as dinner or driving, as well as media-free locations at home, such as bedrooms.

- Have ongoing communication about online citizenship and safety, including treating others with respect online and offline."[15]

How do these recommendations compare with your children's screen usage? Most parents will find that their children are far above the recommendations. Being aware of the problem is the first step in making some improvements.

If your children are old enough, discuss reasonable limits on media and how your family will monitor and set those limits. What limits did you decide to set?

_____

_____

_____

Talking About the Birds and the Bees

One more thing on your to-do list as a parent ... talk to your kids about relationships, love and sex! Did you know that experts recommend the conversation should be started by age five and that by age seven children should have a basic understanding about the facts of reproduction? Children with this information are less likely to be the victims of sexual abuse.

Starting the Conversation

By starting the dialog when your children are young, it's easier to continue it as they grow older. Although you may be uncomfortable discussing the basics of sex with your young children, they typically are not embarrassed. One way to get started is to read an age appropriate book together.

Plan to have many small talks over the years.

There are many excellent books on sexuality for all age groups. You can find a number of these books on the Priceless Parenting website: PricelessParenting.com/BooksOnSexuality

Most young children are interested in their bodies and the differences between boys and girls. Understanding private parts and who has a right to touch or see them is important information for kids to know.

You can find helpful resources on Amy Lang's site BirdsAndBeesAndKids.com. She offers practical ideas in articles like "How To Talk To Kids Who Are Playing Doctor"[16]. You'll also find free videos on how to talk to your kids about sex.

Continuing the Conversation

As children reach puberty, they need information about the changes their bodies will be going through. Although some children will learn this information in school, it's still important for you to be part of the conversation.

When your children have questions or concerns, you want them to be able to come to you. They will be more comfortable approaching you if you have been engaged in an ongoing dialog over the years.

Discussing Your Values About Sexuality

By clarifying your own values and beliefs about sexuality and relationships, you are in a better position to discuss these issues with your children. You can help prepare your children to make better decisions in their relationships by discussing your values.

It's up to you to bring up the conversation about relationships and sex. Without enough information teens often underestimate the likelihood of contracting a sexually transmitted disease or becoming pregnant.

Warning Your Kids About Pornography

You want to alert your kids to pornography before they accidentally see it. It's a good idea to bring the topic up by the time they are 6-years-old.

You can describe porn as pictures or videos of people with little or no clothes on engaged in sexual behavior. Let your kids know that if they see these types of pictures or videos it will probably feel wrong.

Also let them know that if they see porn, you'd like them to look away and then tell you. Reassure them that they won't be in trouble. You want to know so that you can help them.

Having a conversation about porn is challenging for most parents. Kristen Jenson and Gail Poyner have made it easier with their book Good Pictures, Bad Pictures[17]. It's a story of a mom talking to her son about pornography. The book is designed to be read together with 5 to 12-year-old kids. It discusses how kids can get addicted to porn and how they can avoid this. There is also a version of this book for preschoolers, Good Pictures, Bad Pictures Jr[18].

If your kids have their own phones, let them know that sexting is legally considered child pornography. Be sure to discuss the fact that once a picture is sent, it is around forever. That picture may be passed around to many others with devastating results.

What discussions have you had or want to have with your children on relationships, sex, birth control, abstinence or pornography?

_____

_____

_____

Protecting Your Kids from Sexual Abuse

Kids who experience sexual abuse are traumatized in ways that can take years or even decades to overcome. This is why you want to do everything you possibly can to prevent this tragedy.

Understanding Likely Perpetrators

Before you can effectively protect your kids, it's helpful to know some facts. How likely are they to be sexually abused? Who is most likely to be a perpetrator? What makes children more likely to become victims?

According to research presented on Darkness to Light, d2l.org,

- 10% of children in the U.S. are sexually abused by the time they are 18
- Over 90% of the time the perpetrator is someone known by the child or family
- Nearly 40% are abused by older or larger children

A sexual abuser is someone most likely known to your family.

While it might feel better to think that only a stranger would sexually abuse your child, nine times out of ten it's someone you know. The vast majority of abuse occurs when the perpetrator and the child are alone together. Keeping this in mind can help you make wise choices about who is left alone with your children.

If you are a mom who does not live with your kids' father, you need to be especially careful about who you bring into your home. Men who are not related to the children are far more likely to sexually abuse them.

Older Kids Abusing Younger Kids

How about the fact that 40% of sexual abuse is caused by older or larger children? It's important to realize that the abuser is not always an adult. This puts a different twist on keeping your kids safe.

Kids can be abused by older siblings, cousins or neighbors. They can also be abused by older children who are in a babysitter role.

You probably have warned your kids to tell you if anyone hurts them. They also need to know that when their private parts are touched it can feel good. So sexual abuse may not hurt and that can be confusing or embarrassing for kids. They should know that it can feel good but that they are the only ones who should be touching their privates and only when alone.

Adults who sexually abuse kids may tell the children that it's their secret. They will warn the kids not to tell anyone. Talk to your kids about the difference between good secrets and bad secrets.

Trusting Your Gut

If you have an uncomfortable feeling about leaving your kids with someone, trust your intuition. You probably can override your uneasiness by logically explaining to yourself why this person should be fine with your kids. Avoid this mistake.

Joelle Casteix was sexually abused as a teen by one of her teachers. Her experience has compelled her work in helping prevent and expose child sexual abuse. In her book, The Well-Armored Child: A Parent's Guide to Preventing Sexual Abuse, she writes "Predators love it when we don't listen to our gut. Why? Because when we see a predator in action, we rationalize the actions and make excuses. Thus we might overlook what are in fact the first stages of grooming – the little actions that strike us as a bit odd."[19]

There is a lot you can do to protect your kids from sexual abuse. It's absolutely worth your effort to educate yourself and your kids.

What steps will you take to protect your kids from sexual abuse?

_____

_____

_____

_____

Making Time to be Together

Being able to spend fun times together with your children is part of what makes being a parent so rewarding. It also shows your children how important they are to you. However, it can be challenging taking time to have fun.

Postponing the Most Important Things

Your days can easily be filled to overflowing with all the tasks that are required to keep your family running: making meals, doing dishes, driving your kids to activities, washing clothes and working.

Spending fun time together creates wonderful memories.

While these are certainly not the most important things in your life, they can quickly take over most of your time. It's easy to say things like:

- "I'll play a game with the kids tomorrow."
- "We'll go for a bike ride together soon."
- "I'll bake some cookies with them when I have more time."

The things that are the most important to you are also often the ones that are the easiest to postpone. The problem is that sometimes you delay so long that you miss the opportunity.

Your children will not want to have a tea party or play catch with you forever. They quickly grow up. If you want to share special times with your children, you must intentionally carve out the time to do these things.

At the end of your life, what do you want your children to remember about you? Certainly I don't want my kids' strongest memory to be "Mom always kept the bathrooms really clean!" However, if I want my kids to remember special times we shared together, then I need to take time today to play with them, listen to them and be there for them.

Carving Out Daily Time Together

Children need your ongoing attention. If you don't give them enough attention, they may misbehave just to get some attention.

One mom explained when she came home from work each day the first thing she did was change into more comfortable clothes. Her 4-year-old son typically managed to get in trouble or throw a tantrum while she was changing her clothes.

She decided to try a new routine. When she came home, she spent a few minutes playing with him before she changed her clothes. This made a huge, positive difference!

What activities do you most enjoy doing with your children?

_____

_____

_____

_____

Discuss with your children something special they would like to do. What do they want to do and when will you do it?

_____

_____

_____

_____

Chapter 2: Parenting Behaviors to Avoid

Priceless® Parenting

Some parenting techniques may work well in the short term but lead to long term problems. This chapter reviews some of the parenting behaviors that are best to avoid.

Avoiding Negative Techniques

You've undoubtedly heard the saying "The only person you can change is yourself." It's both wise and true! The part not mentioned is that changing your behavior does affect others. When you positively change your behavior, you may be amazed at the equally positive changes in your children's behavior.

One way you can make positive changes in your parenting is to stop certain behaviors. It is easy to get into the habit of using negative techniques, like yelling, in response to your children's misbehavior. However, by refraining from yelling, hitting, nagging and lecturing, you will see wonderful changes in your relationship with your children.

"I've learned that people will forget what you said, people will forget what you did, but people will never forget how you made them feel."
-- Maya Angelou

Short-Term Success With Long-Term Problems

This chapter explores common parenting behaviors that are best to avoid. Some of these behaviors, like bribing children, are very tempting since they may immediately correct a behavior. However, the long-term results are poor.

When you use a negative technique to try to change your children's behavior, it often works in the short-term but typically doesn't leave you feeling good. When you set limits on your kids' behavior while treating them with respect, they feel appreciated and loved. You also model how to treat others with respect.

Think back to your last interaction with your children when you were dealing with a problem.

- How do you think they felt afterwards?

- How did you feel?

- Is there a different way you'd like to handle a situation like this in the future?

If you want to build warm, loving relationships with your children, pay attention to these feelings for guidance. Negative approaches often leave both you and your children feeling bad.

Seeking Revenge Through Punishment

Punishment and discipline represent two very different beliefs about how to best respond to children's misbehavior. Discipline's goal is to help children learn from their mistakes. Punishment's goal is to have children suffer as a way of preventing this type of behavior in the future.

Discipline will eventually come from inside the children. This self-discipline allows your children to make good choices even when you're not around.

Developing self-discipline is a key to success.

Punishment - involves shame, blame, pain

- Retribution is achieved through suffering, pain or loss

- Belief that more severe punishment will make it less likely for the behavior to occur again

- Punishment remains the same no matter what the offense

- Punishment comes from outside the child

- Children learn to fear and resent authority

Discipline - involves thinking, learning, taking responsibility

- Natural or logical consequences as a result of misbehavior

- The certainty, not the severity, of the consequence matters

- Discipline is determined based on how to make amends for the mistake

- Teaches children about taking responsibility for their decisions and actions

- Discipline eventually comes from inside the child

The techniques in this chapter involve punishment rather than discipline. You want to avoid responding to your kids by punishing them. Punishment often leads to kids getting sneakier at hiding their transgressions rather than improving their behavior.

Hitting Children

Parents who spank or hit their kids may do so because it temporarily stops a behavior. While hitting children may stop a behavior, there are longer term negative effects including:

- Increasing children's aggression

- Teaching children to hit others

- Deteriorating children's relationship with their parents

Learn ways to set limits without resorting to hitting.

While it is very important for you to set limits with your children, it should be done in a way that helps your children learn from their mistakes. These ideas will be explored more in the next chapter.

Better Ways to Express Your Anger

An exasperated dad of a 12-year-old boy told me "I wish I could just beat him! That would straighten him out." He explained that as a child he had been beaten and he quickly learned not to misbehave. His son had just been suspended from school that day for fighting and he was at wits end trying to figure out how to deal with this boy's behavior.

When you're experiencing this level of challenge and frustration with your child, it's time to get some outside help. Hitting your child is definitely not the answer.

In Dr. Michael Bradley's book, Crazy-Stressed, he writes, "When it comes to anger, model *narrating* it, not *becoming* it. That means no hitting, threatening, or belittling. Ever. Hurting teens to teach them to not be hurtful teaches only that might (physical or verbal) makes right. What can feel very powerful to your brain can look very weak to your kid and cost you dearly in respect currency. Worse, the real issues (such as drugs or sex) get buried in the cage match of a power contest. Getting hurtful with a teenager is playing in her stadium - you're giving her the home field advantage of suggesting that rage is a way of solving problems. Remember that she is willing to get crazier than you. Don't go there."[1]

It is OK to tell your children how angry you are. In fact, you can even let them know you are too angry to deal with them right now. You can send them to their rooms and let them know you'll stop by when you've had a chance to calm down.

Yelling at Children

When parents attending my classes talk about which of their behaviors they'd most like to change, the most common response is that they'd like to stop yelling at their kids. It is very natural to yell when you're angry; nobody must teach you how to do that!

Begging for Ice Cream

One mom described how annoyed she became while driving her 10-year-old son to Baskin Robbins to order cake for his upcoming birthday party. Her son started pleading with her to get an ice cream cone at Baskin Robbins. Mom said he couldn't have one since he had just had ice cream yesterday.

Ranting and raving leaves everyone feeling bad.

He didn't give up hope and instead kept asking her if he could please have an ice cream cone. Completely fed up, she pulled over and stepped out of the car for a few minutes explaining she needed a break from his behavior. After getting back in the car, he soon asked her again about the ice cream!

Feeling quite angry now, she yelled at him for continuing to ask. By the end of her rant, he was crying. Needless to say, this wasn't exactly the pleasant outing she had envisioned.

Alternative Parenting Responses

You don't always do your best parenting in the heat of the moment. The good news is that when you realize you haven't handled a parenting situation in the ideal way, you can reflect on what happened and figure out what you would like to do differently in the future.

Sometimes you're too close to the situation or still too upset to see any alternatives. If this is the case, it can be helpful to ask other parents for ideas. It's always easier to see choices when you're not the parent involved!

What suggestions might you give this mom?

Ideally you are looking for a response that models both self-control and treating others with respect. You also need to be able to follow through with whatever you say you are going to do. For example, you might tell your son if he begs again you will turn around and go home without getting the ice cream cake. Then if he begs again you need to follow through by turning around and going home.

Nagging and Ordering Children Around

It's easy to get in the habit of nagging children and expressing frustration when they don't quickly obey. When you nag your children, the unspoken belief is that unless you give them continual reminders of what they should be doing, they will forget. However, making requests multiple times does not increase the chance your children will do what you are asking; it actually teaches them how to tune you out.

Eliminating Nagging from the Morning Routine

Do you ever find yourself rushing around in the morning desperately trying to get your kids off to school? Feeling rushed and hassled first thing in the morning is not a good way to start!

How can you change your behavior so that mornings feel calm instead of chaotic? It can help to take a step back and look at what needs to get done in the mornings.

Replace nagging with giving children responsibility.

Replacing Nagging and Ordering with Giving Kids Responsibility

One thing that adds to morning stress is when you feel you need to give your kids lots of orders to get them out the door on time:

- "Eat your breakfast."
- "Brush your teeth."
- "Get dressed right now!"
- "Remember to bring your clarinet."

Giving orders presents a couple problems. The first is that it sets up a power struggle if your kids choose not to follow your order. The second is that orders send the unspoken message "You need me to help you remember what to do." This isn't the message you want to be sending!

Instead it's better if you can help your children find their own ways to remember. For example, your children could create a chart of everything that needs to be done each morning and then check the chart to make sure everything is done. Turning more responsibility over to your children can be scary as mistakes will undoubtedly be made. However, children quickly learn from their mistakes and become more competent.

Doing Things for Children that They Can Do for Themselves

When you do things for your children that they are capable of doing, you may feel exhausted and underappreciated. When you expect your children to do things they know how to do, they develop responsibility.

Never mind, I'll do it!

Are you ever frustrated by the lack of speed your children have in getting tasks done? When you are tired of waiting or really need something done right now, you may find yourself saying "Never mind, I'll do it!"

Allow children to do whatever they are capable of doing.

It often takes less time and energy to simply do it yourself. However, when you jump in and do it for them, you steal their opportunity to increase their self-discipline and sense of responsibility.

When you take over for your kids, they may think things like:

- I can get out of doing work if I simply delay long enough.
- Dad is mad at me but at least I don't have to do it.
- I'm kind of lazy.

Since this response isn't sending positive messages to your children, it's something to avoid doing.

Taking Over Tasks Children Can Do

One dad described being so frustrated with his 5-year-old son's slowness in getting dressed that he finally took over and dressed his son. In his anger he scolded his son saying he was acting like a baby and shouldn't need help to get dressed.

What was this boy thinking about himself after being compared to a baby? What thoughts was he having about his dad?

Another approach this dad could have taken was to give his son the choice of getting dressed at home or taking his clothes in a bag and getting dressed at school. This simple technique was first described by Jane Nelsen in her <u>Positive Discipline</u> book. It was something she tried with her own son and it worked so well she shared it![2]

Bribing Children

Why do parents turn to bribing their kids to behave? One reason is that it often gets the desired results right away.

One mom explained how her son was begging her to watch a Star Wars movie that they had bought the previous night. They were planning to watch it as a family the following night but that wasn't soon enough for him! He kept on asking to watch it and proceeded to try to persuade her even when she was on the phone.

Since her phone call was for business and she really needed to complete the conversation, she took a quick break to promise her son cookies if he stopped bugging her. He immediately agreed and stopped nagging her!

Bribing solves a short-term problem while creating a long-term problem.

While she achieved the desired behavior, he learned that nagging her may result in a treat. Do you think he'll try nagging her again?

Whatever behaviors you reward, you can expect to see more of those behaviors in the future.

Increasing the Reward

Another problem with bribing is that it doesn't address the underlying issue. For example, if you are shopping with a young child who is tired, you may be able to use bribery to temporarily get better behavior. However, the poor behavior is likely to quickly return since your child is still tired.

Once while shopping at Trader Joes I overheard a mom struggling with her young daughter who was sitting in the front of their shopping cart. Mom agreed "OK, I'll give you one money." The daughter whined "Nooooo, I want TWO monies!" Mom fished around her purse and handed her a couple coins. The daughter then yelled "That's not enough!" and began crying.

Mom begged her to please stop crying because she really needed to get this shopping done before they could go home. Mom was exasperated as her daughter continued to cry.

If you find yourself begging or bribing your kids to behave, it's time to find some better parenting approaches!

Giving in To Keep Kids Happy

Part of being a parent is setting limits for your kids. Your kids will not be happy with some of those limits. They may whine, beg, pout or become angry.

Giving In To Begging

This is exactly what happened when a dad told his young daughter that he was not buying her candy at the store. As they waited in the line to check out their groceries, she continued to beg him to buy her a candy bar. Finally, he gave up in exasperation exclaiming "Fine you little brat, you can have it!"

Giving in creates short-term happiness and long-term problems.

By giving in to her pleading, she is likely to use this tactic again since it worked. She also learned that her dad is willing to bend his rules to avoid having her make a scene at the store.

Giving In To Anger

Do you ever have trouble keeping limits around your kid's digital device usage? Perhaps you can relate to Erin's situation. Her son loves playing video games. When she tells him it's time to turn it off, he gets angry so she often lets him play a little longer.

Even though Erin feels he is spending too much time on video games, she hates dealing with his crankiness when it's time to turn it off. It's easier at the moment to give him a little more time.

Giving In To Avoid Conflict

Another mom described her son's limited food preferences. She hated fighting with him over what he would eat. He likes pizza, pasta, hot dogs and hamburgers so that's what he has for dinner every night.

She knows this isn't a healthy diet for him. However, it keeps him from complaining about the food.

When you strive to keep your kids happy, they miss out on learning to handle their more difficult emotions. You may also be sacrificing what is healthy for them in the long-term for short-term peacefulness.

Threatening or Scaring Children

Another way to get kids to quickly change their behavior is to threaten them. While it may work, you erode their trust when you make threats like "If you don't shape up I'm just going to leave you here!"

What Do Children Learn from Threats?

One Mom wrote that her 4-year-old daughter did not want to put on her shoes so they could leave McDonalds when it was time to go. She solved the problem by telling her daughter "That's fine. I'll leave you here and the hobos will come and take you away." Her daughter immediately got her shoes on!

Threatening children weakens their trust.

While scaring kids may work in the short-term, in the long-term the consequences aren't so desirable. Since you really can't abandon them at McDonalds, children learn you won't necessarily follow through on what you say.

Replacing Threats with Promises

Julie was irritated with her preschool daughter after she pitched fit for 45 minutes upon hearing that her little brother was going swimming while she was at preschool. When Julie was completely fed up with the whining and crying, she threatened to let her daughter sit in her room all day missing both preschool and a dance class. Her daughter stopped crying and got ready for school.

In this case, the threat got the girl to stop her tantrum. But what if she had continued? Does Julie really want her daughter to have the choice of skipping school? Probably not.

The problem with threats is that you normally make them when you are angry and therefore threaten things that you really don't want to carry through on. Instead of using a threat, Julie could have used a promise when her daughter started protesting like "I know you are upset that you can't go swimming today. I'll be happy to take you swimming next week if I don't use up that energy listening to you whining and crying."

You want your children to be able to trust that you will follow through on what you say. So you want to avoid threats made in anger since those threats tend to be extreme and not well-thought-out. It is far better to choose promises you'd be happy to fulfill rather than angry threats that will deteriorate your relationship with your children.

Lecturing and Over Explaining

When you feel strongly about a topic, it's easy to launch into a lecture. Unfortunately, lecturing is not very effective in changing behavior.

For example, parents who feel passionate about their children trying hard in school may lecture them about the importance of studying hard. To the parents giving the lecture, it may feel like progress is being made. However, they may be very disappointed to find that their children still aren't getting their homework done even after carefully explaining the importance of doing homework!

Use fewer words to get better results.

Lecturing is not a Dialog

Lecturing is one-sided. You talk, your children listen, or at least pretend to listen! You tell your kids what you believe on a topic. However, since this isn't a discussion, your children don't usually get to voice their opinions and ideas.

At the end of a lecture, you may think your children will now behave differently. If your children haven't responded, it's not clear how they intend to change or not change their behavior.

When giving the lecture, you may take the stance of being unquestionably correct. When that's the case, there is no room for questions or dialog because there is only one right answer.

Children are more committed to changing their behavior when they've been involved with the decision. Lectures don't allow this buy-in.

Over Explaining Provides Attention

When you explain to your children at length about why a certain behavior is not appropriate, you are giving children lots of attention. Attention tends to reinforce behaviors so you may be encouraging the very behavior you want to stop!

One day I saw a couple was trying to convince their 5-year-old daughter to get in the car because it was time to leave the park. This girl did not want to go home.

Her parents carefully explained why they needed to go home. I walked by 30 minutes later and they were still explaining to her why they needed to go!

Battling Over Food

Meals are perfect for gathering your family together. Making meal times pleasant, instead of a battle ground, will greatly improve the precious time you spend together.

Avoiding Power Struggles Around Eating

I heard a 9-year-old girl ask her dad "Why are you the boss of what I eat?" Her dad was carefully monitoring how much she was eating and encouraging her to eat more to earn dessert.

Food battles make sharing meals together unpleasant.

This type of battle takes a toll on relationships plus makes meal time unpleasant. It is your job to provide healthy food and to teach your children why their bodies need healthy food. However, it is your children's job to decide what to eat and how much to eat.

If you want to set limits around food, tell your kids what you are going to do or give them choices. For example:

- "You're welcome to have the noodles I'm making for lunch or you can make yourself a sandwich."

- "I've put out carrots and grapes. Help yourself to as much of these as you'd like before dinner is ready."

- "We'll be leaving the restaurant in 5 minutes. Finish eating as much as you want so you're not hungry before we eat again."

Be sure the choices you give are all ones that you would be happy with your child selecting.

Catering to Food Preferences

You can accidentally encourage picky eating by doing things like:

- Buying a single brand – like only Oroweat 12 Grain bread

- Taking special meals for your kids to someone else's house

- Serving only food your children already like.

One high school girl reported she finally started trying new food when she took a trip with her high school class to Europe. She commented that being hungry was a very good motivator!

Arguing Over Homework

Do your children struggle to get their homework done each day? Do they outright refuse to do it sometimes? If you are in the habit of struggling with your kids over homework, it's no fun for anyone.

The good news is you can change these dynamics! One school counselor reported that she saw many kids who refused to do their homework. When she asked what they would do if their parents left homework up to them, almost all the kids replied they would do their homework. They explained they did not want to disappoint their teachers, miss their recess time or be embarrassed by not having it done.

Let your kids take responsibility for their homework.

When your kids focus on resisting you, they can't feel these internal motivations. How can you remove your children's resistance and increase the likelihood of their homework getting done?

Giving Your Kids Responsibility for Their Homework

Remove yourself from the equation by saying something like, "I realize that when I try to make you do your homework both of us end up feeling bad. From now on I'm going to leave your homework up to you. I have faith that you can work out any issues around getting your homework done with your teacher. I want you to be successful in school so you are welcome to use the TV or computer after your homework is done. However, it's up to you to decide when and if you do your homework."

Asking questions is another way to help your child think through the possible consequences.

- "How will you respond when your teacher asks you for your homework?"

- "What does your teacher do when kids don't have their homework done?"

- "Does your homework have any effect on your grade? What grade would you like to have?"

It's critical to ask these questions with calm curiosity instead of in anger. By doing this you leave the responsibility of figuring out how to handle homework with your child.

Saying "I told you so!" or "Because I said so!"

When you say things like "I told you so!", you are rubbing salt in the wound. If your children are suffering because they failed to follow your advice, it is far better to show compassion for their pain.

"Didn't I tell you this would happen?"

A young boy was walking home with his mother from school. He tripped on the bottom of his pants, fell, skinned his knee and burst into tears. His mother reminded him "I told you this would happen! Those pants are too long for you."

When you've been proven correct, don't mention it.

Her son would have felt more understood if she showed compassion. Instead she could have given him a hug saying something like "Ow! That really hurt.". Showing compassion would have put her on the same side of the problem as her son with his bad decision on the other side. He already had the natural consequence of skinning his knee which taught him the problem with wearing pants that are too long.

"Because I said so!"

Lucy angrily recalled a turning point in her relationship with her mom over 50 years ago. She was graduating from 9th grade and asked her mother if after the graduation ceremony she could spend the afternoon at a lake with some of her girlfriends. One of the other mothers was driving them to the lake and bringing lunch.

Her mom replied, "You're not going." When Lucy asked her mom why she couldn't go, her response was "Because I said so."

Lucy was enraged with her mother's explanation. She angrily told her mother that she planned to go to the lake with her friends despite the fact her mother told her she couldn't go. When her mother asked for an explanation, Lucy replied "Because I said so." Lucy did go to the lake with her friends that day. Her relationship with her mother remained cool and unaffectionate for many years.

When you declare to your children something will or will not happen "because I said so", you are using your authority to end the discussion. A better approach is to carefully listen to your child's request and ask questions to address any concerns you have before deciding. Providing respectful, thoughtful explanations for decisions helps maintain good relationships with your children even if the decision isn't the one they wanted.

Reacting Before Understanding

It's easy to react to your children's behavior before you really understand why they did or said something. Below is an example of this type of reaction along with an idea for a better approach.

A mom told the story of driving her 5-year-old son, Nick, home from school one day when he announced, "John is an ass!" Taken aback by this name calling, she responded to Nick "Good boys do not use language like that. You should never call anyone that name."

She then asked Nick why he said that. Nick explained that John was always asking him to play every day. She replied "That's a really nice thing that John is doing. You should be happy that he wants to play with you." That remark shutdown the conversation and Nick was now mad both at John and his mom.

"Seek first to understand and then to be understood."
~ Stephen R. Covey

Let's take a step back and see how this might have played out differently. In the dialog below, Mom ignores the inappropriate language and avoids telling Nick that he should be happy that John is asking him to play.

Nick: "John is an ass!"

Mom: "You sound really angry."

Nick: "Yeah, he is always asking me to play with him every day."

Mom: "Why is that a problem?"

Nick: "Because sometimes I'm already playing a game with someone else and I don't want to stop in the middle of it."

Mom: "John wants you to stop what you are playing and play with him."

Nick: "Yeah, but I don't want to."

Mom is now making headway in understanding why Nick is feeling angry with John. She's also helping Nick gain insight into the underlying issues. Once they truly understand the situation, they can brainstorm possible solutions.

Mom can always go back later and address Nick's choice of words. When Nick is calm, he'll be in a better frame of mind for considering other ways he could express his anger.

Breaking Promises

Has your child ever accusingly said, "But you promised!"? Did you break a promise or did your child misinterpret a statement as a promise when no promise was intended?

Being intentional about what is a promise and what is not can be helpful in avoiding misunderstandings. Once you make a promise, it is important to follow through with whatever you promised.

Remembering Broken Promises

People remember broken promises for years, especially if it was an emotional event. An older woman recalled being at a pool and being afraid of going down the slide. Her dad was in the water and promised her that he would catch her. However, when she came sliding down, he didn't catch her.

She popped right up after being under water. She felt deceived but realized that her dad wanted her to learn that she could do it. Years later she clearly remembers that broken promise and her feelings of being betrayed.

Only make promises you are sure you can keep.

Recovering From a Broken Promise

What do you do when you've broken a promise to your child and now your child is upset? Rick explained that he had promised his 12-year-old son that he would play a game of cribbage with him that night. However, time slipped by and it was time for bed before they got to play the game.

When his son realized they weren't going to be able to play the game that night, he was angry. Rick acknowledged his feelings and apologized. "I can see you are angry that we don't have time to play cribbage tonight. I'm sorry I didn't realize how late it was. Let's set an alarm to go off tomorrow night at 7:00 so that we remember to play the game then."

Acknowledging his feelings and apologizing calmed his son down. His reaction would have been different had Rick said "You're getting upset for nothing! I'll play cribbage with you tomorrow night." He probably would have gotten even more upset because his dad would have not only broken his promise but also dismissed his feelings.

Spending in Ways that Create Entitled Kids

Are your kids begging you to buy things? If so, the marketers are being effective in teaching your children one of the best ways to get you to break down and buy it - beg! Advertisers teach kids to beg because they've proven begging works.

You also may be unintentionally fueling the begging by giving in. In her book, Give Me, Get Me, Buy Me!, Donna Corwin explains her role. "Entitled children are created, not born. I became a Give Me, Get Me, Buy Me parent early on. Not wanting to deprive my princess of anything, I indulged her until she started to get used to the good life. In fact, I trained her so well that, like Pavlov's dog, when we entered a shopping mall, she didn't start to salivate or bark, but she did whine incessantly."[3]

Giving into begging ultimately hurts your kids.

Influencing Your Spending

Marketers are keenly aware that kids have a significant influence on their parents spending. From the brand of macaroni and cheese to where to go on vacation, children have a big say. No wonder businesses are focused on turning children into voracious consumers.

The documentary "Consuming Kids: The Commercialization of Childhood" explores how marketers work their magic with children. According to Gary Ruskin, "Corporate marketers have actually studied the whole nagging phenomenon - which corporations do nagging better - and they provide advice to corporations about what kinds of tantrums work better."[4]

Selling to Your Children

Marketers are not interested in what's best for your children. They're interested in helping children want what they have to sell - pop, sugared cereals, candy, fast food, toys and other treats.

Since advertising works by creating a need that can be fulfilled by a product, it often highlights some inadequacy or common fear. While these underlying messages are subtle, they can certainly contribute to feelings of not having enough or not being enough.

When you choose to buy something for your children, make sure it's for good reasons – not to stop their whining.

Sneaking, Spying or Snooping

You may have a legitimate concern which is leading you to want to sneak, spy or snoop on your kids. If this is the case, consider how you can be upfront with your kids instead of going behind their backs.

One problem with sneaking around is that it breaks down trust in relationships. Another problem is that if you find something wrong it's awkward to bring it up to your child. Your concern will be tainted by how you came up with this information.

Tell your kids what you are going to do so you don't have to sneak, spy or snoop.

Establishing Rules and Expectations

You are responsible for keeping your family safe. This requires knowing what is in your home. Your children's rights to privacy need to be balanced with your responsibility to keep them safe.

You can have rules about what is allowed in your house. For example, you may tell your kids that you do not allow illegal drugs in your house. You also let them know that you reserve the right to go into their rooms if you believe there may be drugs.

One mom was concerned about her daughters' use of their cellphones. She told them that she would be randomly checking their phones. The rule was when she asked them for their phones, they needed to hand the phone over immediately.

One day she was doing a random check and saw her daughter was sending bullying messages to another girl. She was able to talk to her daughter about it including how she would make amends for this bullying. It was easier for her to hold her daughter accountable because she was open about how she would be checking her phone.

It is appropriate to have some level of monitoring of your kids' digital devices. Tell them upfront what type of monitoring tools you will be using so that there are no surprises.

Digital devices provide many opportunities for your kids to interact with people who may not have their best interests at heart. You want to avoid being one of the parents who learns about a child's illegal online activities when the police show up at your door.

Shaming Publicly or Privately

Do you remember being scolded with "Shame on you!" growing up? Perhaps it was followed with "You should know better than that!" How did it make you feel? Probably pretty bad.

For many generations shame has been a primary parenting tool. Brené Brown explains the power of using shame in <u>The Gifts of Imperfect Parenting</u>. "The truth is you can change a child's behavior on a dime with shame. For this simple reason - children experience shame as the threat of being unlovable. And so it's not very difficult to use shame to turn their behaviors around."[5]

> "Shame is the intensely painful feeling or experience of believing that we are flawed and therefore unworthy of love and belonging."
> ~ Brené Brown

So if it's effective why not use it? Because it damages your children's feelings of self-worth.

How are kids shamed? Unfortunately, there are plenty of examples.

- Telling children that they are bad, lazy, stupid, liar, fat, ugly

- Threatening kids that they are going to be put up for adoption

- Forcing kids to hold a sign in public stating things like "I am a thief. Do not trust me."

- Cutting a child's hair in a way that encourages others to make fun of that child

- Hitting children including paddling kids at school

- Posting videos or pictures of kids online with the purpose of shaming them

- Letting your kids know that they need to achieve a certain level of success to be a worthy member of your family (e.g. earn a PhD, become a politician, doctor, lawyer)

- Suspending a child from school (underlying message is that you are so bad, we don't even want you here)

Shaming is harmful because it damages a child's feelings of self-worth. The next chapter explores approaches that are far better than shaming in response to children's behavior.

Chapter 3: Responding Positively to Misbehavior

When you respond to your children's misbehavior in a new way, you usually get different results. This chapter guides you through focusing on one problem at a time and trying new ways of handling it.

Choosing New Approaches

The last chapter examined parenting behaviors to avoid. This chapter presents various parenting ideas to try instead.

Parents frequently state that what works well with one child does not work for another child. This is so true! Since each of your children are different, you will need to figure out what works best with each child.

Making mistakes is part of learning.

Being Patient with Yourself

Parenting can be difficult. Your children will challenge you and cause you to grow in ways you never imagined before having kids. Give yourself credit for working on improving your parenting.

Try to not be too hard on yourself if you don't handle a parenting situation ideally. Instead, dedicate yourself to figuring out a better approach for next time. Changing your own behavior takes time, dedication and plenty of practice.

Taking parenting classes or reading books should increase your skills while leaving you feeling better about your parenting, not worse. While there isn't one parenting technique that will magically work with all children, there are many approaches that work extremely well.

Focusing On One Problem at a Time

On the next page you will find the Challenging Behavior Worksheet. This worksheet guides you through tracking one problem behavior at a time.

You can make copies of this worksheet or use a notebook to record this information. If you would like to print out extra copies, you can find this document online at

http://www.PricelessParenting.com/documents/cbw.pdf

Use the ideas in the rest of this chapter to figure out new approaches in responding to these challenging behaviors.

Challenging Behavior Worksheet

What is one of your children's behaviors that you currently find difficult?

_____

_____

_____

How do you typically respond to this behavior?

_____

_____

_____

What new response will you try?

_____

_____

_____

What was the result of using this new response?

_____

_____

_____

Asking Your Children for Ideas

Your children may have some very good ideas about why they are choosing to behave in ways that you find challenging. If they are old enough, begin by asking them for their thoughts on this. After you understand their motivations, explain your concerns with the behavior.

Finally ask your children for ideas on how to satisfy both their needs and yours. You might just be surprised at what they say!

Helping Tweens and Teens Think Through Their Behavior

Once children are teens, many parents ground their kids as a consequence for misbehavior. The hope is that by requiring teens to be home instead of with friends, teens will learn to make better choices. However, teens are probably spending their time thinking about how to not get caught in the future!

The person who has the problem is often the best person to figure out the solution.

An approach which is more likely to encourage teens to learn from a poor choice is to ask them to write about it. James explained how he used this technique with his son, Tim. Tim had gone to the theater with friends but discovered the movie was sold out. They walked to a nearby park and hung out. James was upset because Tim failed to update him. He worried when Tim didn't come home after the movie.

Instead of grounding him, James asked Tim to write about the situation answering questions like:

- What was the sequence of events that happened?
- What influenced your actions?
- What would you do differently next time?
- What type of amends do you think you should make?

James explained that he would decide on any further consequences based on Tim's reflection. Struggling to write down the answers to these types of tough questions can help teens learn from their poor choices. While they may be tempted to blame others for their actions, the goal of this exercise is for them to realize their own role in the situation and take responsibility.

What are your kids' ideas for changing their challenging behavior?

Letting Children Solve Their Own Problems

When you allow your children to solve their own problems, you help them realize how capable and creative they are. They also learn to figure out how to handle difficult situations by themselves.

Christine Hohlbaum is the author of <u>S.A.H.M. I Am: Tales of a Stay-at-Home Mom in Europe</u>. She wrote about her success in allowing her kids to solve their own problems using ideas from a Priceless Parenting class:

'Fresh off Lesson #3 from today's parenting course, I jumped into it with vigor.

"I'm bored!" my son whined. "Oh, what are you going to do?" I asked. He was stunned.

When children are bored, it's their problem not yours!

Normally, I offer helpful hints, tips and tricks to avoid the Boredom Monster. After he recovered from his initial shock, my son said, "I think I'll call Anton." He quickly got distracted with something his sister was doing, then proudly announced 30 minutes later that he decided now would be a good time to call his friend. They made a playdate. After a quick peck on the cheek, he was out the door.

My daughter, who tends to challenge me wherever I go, looked me squarely in the eye and said, "I'm doing the rest of my homework after dance class." She laid out a sensible plan. "Sounds like you know what you are doing!" was all I said. Another stunned silence ensued. No bickering? Commanding? Bossing around? I smiled sweetly and wished her good luck. My daughter looked about her, put on her shoes, and left for Hip Hop.

Fast-forward a few hours. The kids came home. My daughter dilly-dallied. It started to get late.

"Oh, didn't you say you were going to read out loud?" She claimed she already had. When I reminded her she had said she would do so in front of her father, she had nowhere to go. "Are you going to read now or after your shower?" She started to squirm. I could tell my calm, question-based parenting was started to sink in. It really is her responsibility to make certain things get done in her life.'[1]

Could allowing your children to solve their own problems help?

Allowing Natural Consequences to Teach

The older your children become the more natural consequences will shape their behavior. The most difficult part may be not interfering with natural consequences by rescuing your children.

When your children are experiencing natural consequences, it is always good to show genuine compassion. It is important to avoid saying things like "Didn't I tell you this would happen?"

Suffering Natural Consequences

Here are some examples of natural consequences:

- Your child decides not to take a coat and later complains about being cold.

- Your child forgets to turn in homework and the teacher takes away points.

- Your child stays up late and is tired the next day.

- Your child forgets to bring his baseball mitt to practice so must watch instead of participating.

- Your child waits until the last minute to complete a school assignment and is stressed trying to get it done in time.

Your kids learn simply by experiencing these natural consequences.

Natural consequences work well if you avoid interfering.

Pointing Out Possible Natural Consequences

Frances told a story about her 15-year-old daughter announcing one evening that she had decided to start smoking. Frances resisted the urge to share that she didn't think this was a good idea. Instead she replied, "I hope smoking doesn't interfere with your singing."

The next morning when her daughter came down for breakfast she declared that she had decided against smoking because she really wanted to have the best singing voice possible. Frances was thrilled that she had changed her mind!

What is the natural consequence of your child's challenging behavior?

Choosing Appropriate Consequences

The goal of discipline is to help children learn from their mistakes. The goal is not to serve as retribution to make them pay for the mistake. Sometimes there are no natural consequences. In these situations, a logical consequence may be appropriate.

Choosing Logical Consequences

In her book Kids Are Worth It, Barbara Coloroso explains that consequences should ideally be:[2]

Discipline: comes from Latin disciplina meaning teaching or learning

- Reasonable: The consequence relates to the behavior and is not too severe.

- Simple: The consequence is obvious and can be delivered easily and quickly.

- Valuable: The consequence allows the child to learn from the mistake and make amends.

- Practical: The consequence is achievable and makes sense given the child's age and behavior.

Some things to consider include:

- What can my child do to help make amends for the mistake?

- How can a consequence help my child make better choices?

- How can I use empathy so my child is in a thinking state?

Children can be asked what they think is a reasonable consequence. Involving them makes it more likely to have a positive outcome.

Showing Your Disappointment

Sometimes expressing your disappointment is all the consequence that is needed. For example, if your child takes a piece of cake without asking, you may only need to say, "I'm very disappointed that you took that piece of cake without asking because I was planning to bring it to the school meeting."

What logical consequence could help your kids make better choices?

Finding Solutions Instead of Issuing Consequences

Whenever possible it's best to find a solution to a problem behavior rather than issue a consequence. The goal of solutions is to solve the problem once and for all.

Running Away When It's Time to Leave

When Emma came to pick Avery up from preschool, Avery decided to hide under the table. Emma couldn't coax Avery to come out so she tried reaching under the table to grab Avery's arm but Avery scooted away.

Focusing on solutions sends kids the message that you believe they are capable of better behavior.

Avery was clearly having a good time playing this little keep-away game and Emma was getting more upset by the minute. Finally, one of the teachers helped get Avery out from under the table.

When Emma got home, she told Avery how angry she was with her behavior, spanked her and put her in her room. How could she have worked towards a solution instead of just punishing Avery?

She might have tried practicing the correct behavior with Avery at home in pretend situations. Or perhaps she could change her pick up routine by immediately taking Avery's hand rather than first engaging with other parents in conversation. When you start thinking about solutions to a problem, a lot of possibilities open up.

Forgetting to Call When Staying Late After School

A mom explained how worried and angry she was when her son did not come home from school one day and failed to let her know where he was. Although he has a cellphone, he forgot to call and let her know he was staying after school to work on a project. When he came home, she told him the consequence for his forgetting to call was that he would not be able to watch TV for a week.

How would this situation be different if instead of issuing a consequence, they looked for a solution? Perhaps he could set an alarm on his cellphone for five minutes after school ends to remind him to call if he wasn't coming straight home. Or he could write his after-school plans on a calendar at home. He could also leave a note on the kitchen table in the morning if he planned to stay late.

What are possible solutions for your child's challenging behavior?

Resolving Conflicts Using Collaborative & Proactive Solutions

While it is tempting to try to force children to behave using punishments or rewards, these attempts often fail. Children realize that you are trying to control their behavior and may respond by doing just the opposite of what you'd like.

Dr. Ross Greene's Collaborative & Proactive Solutions[3] process guides you to listen to your children and work together to find a solution. This process works well for situations where you notice a problem and want to bring it up with your child. It consists of three steps:

Somewhere beyond punishments and rewards is a place where we care enough to listen and figure out together how to solve problems.

1. Gathering information to understand your child's concerns

The goal in this first step is to ask your children questions to fully understand their perspective. Keep asking questions until you feel you can stand in their shoes and understand what they are going through. This will take time and patience. Your kids may even need a day to think about their answers.

It's best to start the conversation when the problem behavior is not occurring. Try to bring up it up in a comfortable setting. Having a discussion over a meal or snack can create a more relaxed atmosphere.

Start your conversation in a non-confrontational way. One way to do this is by beginning with "I've noticed that" and ending with "What's up?" For example, "I've noticed that you haven't been too crazy about going to school lately. What's up?"

If your child says, "I don't know", try to figure out why. Does the problem need to be broken into smaller pieces? Does your child need more time to think? Is your child afraid to share information?

After your child answers, check in with yourself to see if you completely understand. If not, ask a clarifying question. You may need many rounds of questions and answers before you feel you understand.

2. Explaining your concerns

After listening to your child, it's your turn to share your concerns. Begin by asking "Is it OK if I share some of my concerns with you?" Most kids will agree since you just listened to them.

However, if they aren't ready, set up a time to continue the conversation. You brought up this conversation because of significant concerns, so you don't want to just drop it.

Your concerns are likely to be around safety, learning, or how your child's behavior is affecting them or someone else. Start with stating facts because these are the least controversial. For example, "Last week you were late to school twice."

After describing the relevant facts, explain why these facts concern you. Your concerns may involve how your child's behavior is affecting themselves or the rest of the family. Be specific. For example, "When you are late to school, the school calls us to acknowledge that you were late. I feel worried because I don't know if something bad happened to you on the way to school."

If you also have concerns about how this effects your child's learning, add those concerns. The more specific you are with your concerns the more likely you are to find a solution to the problem.

3. Brainstorming possible solutions

Now it's time to ask your child for ideas on how to solve the problem. Write down all the ideas that you both have. When brainstorming do not judge the ideas – that will come later. If you say things like "that won't work" or "how ridiculous", you'll stop the ideas from flowing.

Once you have all the ideas, circle the ones that are realistic and meet both your concerns and your child's concerns. Let your child choose one of the circled ideas to try first. Your child will be more invested in an option that they have selected.

Make sure that the solution you've agreed on is one that you and your child can actually do. You want this solution to set your child up for success not failure.

Set up a time to meet again to review how the idea is working. You may want to meet frequently at the beginning until you know the solution is working. If the solution is not working well, discuss with your child whether there needs to be some adjustment made or if it's time to choose another option.

Could using Collaborative & Proactive Solutions help find an answer?

Shaping the Desired Behaviors

You shape your children's behavior by what you pay attention to. When your child has an ongoing behavioral problem, one way to change the behavior is through shaping.

Psychologist Dr. Kazdin has researched shaping kids' behavior. He's seen great success in using the shaping process described in his book The Kazdin Method for Parenting the Defiant Child.[4]

Reward the desired behavior to see more of it.

How do you shape your child's behavior? It involves five steps:

1. Identify the Behavior You Want to Change

What is the behavior that you want to eliminate? Some examples are:

- Not wanting to practice the piano
- Refusing to eat vegetables
- Dragging his feet in getting ready for school
- Coming home later than expected
- Not listening the first time

2. Define the Behavior You Want Instead

This is what Kazdin refers to as the "Positive Opposite". What is the behavior you want? For the examples above the behaviors you want might be:

- Practicing the piano for 30 minutes daily
- Tasting one bite of the vegetables served
- Being ready for school 5 minutes before actually needing to leave
- Letting you know if he will be late
- Paying attention to your request and doing it the first time

3. Figure Out the Series of Small Steps

Shaping your child's behavior involves starting with your child's current behavior and getting them to take a small step in the right direction. For example, if your child will typically sit at the piano for a minute, hit a couple keys and then leave, that's the starting point. So the next small step might be sitting for two minutes and practicing one song the teacher has assigned.

If your child refuses to eat any vegetables, the first small step might be putting a bite of vegetable on a fork and touching it to his tongue without eating it. The idea is to start with one small step in the right direction and build from there.

If your child is chronically late in getting ready for school, this might be the series of small steps you decide to reinforce one at a time:

- Turning off electronics an hour before bedtime
- Checking what is being served at school for lunch the next day
- Packing a lunch or snacks if desired
- Setting an alarm to get up on time
- Deciding what to wear the night before and laying out clothes
- Putting all necessary items in the backpack the night before
- Placing the backpack by the front door

You reward your child every step of the way. The reward can be a celebratory high five, a sticker, an extra story at bedtime or some other small thing your child enjoys.

While you may balk at rewarding your child for something you think they should already be able to do, it's necessary if you want to change your child's behavior. Once your child has the behavior mastered, you no longer need to reward the behavior.

4. Set Your Child Up for Succeeding at the Behavior

This step involves everything that happens before your child's behavior. For example, when making a request your child is more likely to comply if you are calm, smile, use "please" and a pleasant tone. Being near your child when you make a request is much more effective than shouting from across the room.

Another way to increase your child's likelihood of cooperating is to make it a good-natured challenge. For instance, if your 3-year-old is refusing to get dressed you might say "You're a little young to be dressing yourself so I will help you. Most kids can do this sometime before they turn four, so you'll be able to do it pretty soon."

Your kids love your attention so this is another tool in shaping their behavior. For example, if your child doesn't want to practice the piano, you might agree to sit down with your child while he practices.

You might also use a reward chart to acknowledge whenever your child does the behavior. Reward charts can be extremely effective at shaping the behavior you want. The reward chart is a temporary device for getting your child to focus on the behavior you want through earning small rewards.

For example, we used a reward chart when my son was potty training. There were 5 rows with 7 spaces. Each time he pooped in the toilet, he earned one star in a space. After a row was completed, he got a Matchbox car. After all the rows were completed, we had a "big boy" celebration at Chucky E Cheese's! No more accidents – we were thrilled!

5. Positively Reinforce Your Child After the Behavior

Everyone changes their behavior in response to feedback. The best reinforcement comes by doing it right after your child's behavior, being specific, being enthusiastic and including positive touch. These simple actions will increase the likelihood that your child will repeat the behavior.

After your child successfully does the first small step, you change your response to rewarding the next small step. You keep leading your child one step at a time until they can do the final behavior. While the shaping process takes time, your reward is coming when your child achieves the final behavior you want!

Consider your child's challenging behavior. What is the positive opposite? How can you encourage small steps in the right direction?

Using Short Responses

When you respond to your children's misbehavior using lots of words, you are giving them lots of attention. This may be negative attention but any attention will encourage a behavior to continue. So your goal is to limit the words you use when your children are misbehaving.

For example, a dad described a situation where his daughter was begging him to buy a stuffed bear at the store. He had already told her he wouldn't buy it for her and then she started in with "oh p-l-l-le-e-e-a-s-s-e Daddy, I'll be really good the rest of the day if I can just have it!" Instead of explaining again why he wasn't buying it, he just responded "I know you're disappointed. What was my answer?"

Lots of Words = Lots of Attention

Short responses to behaviors like whining and begging will help extinguish those behaviors. The more attention you pay to a behavior, the more likely you are to see it. Be careful what you reinforce!

Powerful One or Two Word Reminders

Two young boys were goofing around in a grocery store parking lot and not paying attention to the traffic around them. Their dad said, *"parking lot"*. That's all he said. The boys quickly stopped messing around and paid attention to where they were.

One or two-word reminders can be effective while saving you from accidentally launching into a mini-lecture ("How many times do I have to remind you to be careful in parking lots!? There are cars ...").

Some short reminders parents have used include:

- "Coat" (remember to take your coat along)
- "Shoes" (it's time to put your shoes on)
- "Towel" (your wet towel needs to be hung up)

A mom told me that when her daughter forgot to put her dirty dishes in the dishwasher after dinner she would just say *"plate"* and walk away. She said using a one-word reminder was effective and prevented her from ranting at her daughter.

Could a short response be useful in dealing with your child's challenging behavior?

Saying What You Will Do Instead of What They Have To Do

When you tell your children what they must do, you are setting yourself up for a power struggle. When you say what you are going to do, you can certainly make that happened!

Orders: Telling Them What To Do	**Statements: Saying What You Will Do**
"Don't look at me that way!"	"I'll be happy to speak to you when you are looking at me in a respectful way."
"Stop your whining!"	"I'll be happy to listen to you when your voice sounds like mine."
"Pick up your toys."	"You can pick up your toys or I'll pick them up and put them in the Earn Back Box."
"Quit fighting!"	"Your fighting is bothering me so I'm going outside to do some gardening."
"Put your dirty clothes in the laundry basket."	"I'll wash whatever clothes are in the laundry basket."
"Get your shoes on!"	"I'll be waiting for you in the car."

Acting Instead of Giving Orders

One mom described her frustration when her son would start splashing water out of the bathtub. Telling him to stop splashing wasn't working. She finally solved the problem by gently taking him out of the tub and drying him off whenever he started splashing water.

She didn't get angry but instead calmly told him that bath time was over. She reported that he quickly learned to not splash in the tub so he could enjoy more time playing in the water.

Could replacing orders with telling them what you are going to do help?

Asking Once

Have you heard parents say to their child *"How many times do I need to ask you?"* When you ask your kids repeatedly to do something, you train them to expect multiple requests before they need to act.

Expect Action After The First Request

You may unintentionally teach your children not to respond the first time you make a request. If they have learned that they don't need to pay attention to you until you're screaming or counting to three, then they often will wait until this point to respond. If instead you ask only once and expect it be done, your kids are more likely to act on your initial request.

Teach your children to respond on your first request.

For example, suppose you asked your child to pick up the jacket he just tossed on the floor. If your child starts playing with a toy instead of picking up his jacket, one way to guide him is to touch him gently on the shoulders and say, "It's time to hang up your jacket." This will help get his attention while letting him know that you expect him to do what you've asked.

You could also state your expectation saying, "Feel free to play with that toy just as soon as your jacket is hung up." What will you do if your child still doesn't pick up his jacket? There are many possibilities including taking away the toy until the jacket is picked up. By acting instead of simply repeating the request, you are teaching your child to respond the first time you ask.

Listening the First Time

When you teach your children to listen the first time, you are giving them responsibility for remembering and acting. On the other hand, continually reminding your children puts the responsibility back on you.

Suppose your child's library book is due at school tomorrow and you've asked him to put it in his backpack. At this point, it's up to him to act. If he forgets, he won't be able to check another book out of the library. If you can stop yourself from reminding him again, he will learn from the consequences.

If your child tends to not listen the first time, what could you do differently when this happens?

Turning a "No" into a "Yes"

People respond better to hearing "yes" to their requests rather than hearing "no". When you can turn a "no" into a "yes", you can grant your children's requests on your terms.[5]

You can do this by stating the circumstances under which the request will be granted. Below are some examples of saying both no and yes to a request.

"Can I have a cookie?"

- "No, it's almost dinner time."
- "Yes, after dinner you can have a cookie."

Finding a way to say "yes" will produce more positive results.

"Can we get a dog?"

- "No, we're not getting a dog."
- "Yes, when you move to your own place, you can have a dog."

"Can I go over to Sam's house?"

- "No, you need to get your homework done."
- "Yes, feel free to go to Sam's house just as soon as your homework is done."

"Can I watch a movie?"

- "No, it's a school night."
- "Yes, on Friday night you can watch a movie."

"Can I have $10?"

- "No, you've already been given your allowance for the week."
- "Yes, I'd be happy to give you $10 if you mow the yard."

How could responding with a conditional "yes" rather than "no" affect your child's challenging behavior?

Setting Effective Limits

You need to set limits whenever your children's behavior is causing a problem for themselves or someone else. An effective limit causes a decrease in the problem behavior over time.

Observing When Limits Are Not Effective

Many young children will try hitting their parents. Jen described how her daughter started hitting her when she was 9-months-old. Jen was very surprised and responded by calmly saying "no hitting, nice" and rubbing the girl's hand gently on her face. However, she continued hitting and Jen resorted to sternly grabbing her hands and saying, "No hit". This also didn't change her behavior.

By 18-months-old, she was hitting, scratching and pulling hair too! She did this with Jen, her dad and other kids. When she hit Jen now, she immediately said "nice" and rubbed her hand on her mom's face. She's learned something but not what Jen had intended!

When you respond to misbehavior in a way that doesn't effectively set a limit, your children's misbehavior will continue and escalate. In this case, the consequence of hearing "no hitting" and rubbing her mom's face did not discourage the girl from hitting. Instead, it encouraged her to try other behaviors to find the limit.

Expect children to test limits.

Setting Limits by Acting

Ruby told the story of how she was planning to go out to lunch with a couple other moms after picking their kids up from preschool. She was looking forward to enjoying pizza and visiting with her friends.

However, her son wasn't behaving well – he was pushing the other kids, running ahead and not listening. She warned him that if he didn't hold her hand and start behaving that they would go home.

His poor behavior continued so reluctantly Ruby decided to take him home. As she carried him, he started hitting her on the head. She put him down and waited for him to calm down enough to walk himself. By following through and setting a firm limit, her son learned from the consequences of his choices.

Is your child's challenging behavior escalating? How could you set a more effective limit?

Identifying Underlying Emotions

Children need help learning to identify and process their feelings. You can begin teaching them to recognize their emotions by labeling them.

Showing Empathy by Identifying with Emotions

In <u>Raising an Emotionally Intelligent Child</u>, John Gottman describes five steps for emotionally coaching children:[6]

1. Become aware of the child's emotions
2. Recognize the emotion as an opportunity for intimacy and teaching
3. Listen empathetically, validating the child's feelings
4. Help the child find words to label the emotion
5. Set limits while exploring strategies to solve the problem at hand.

Show empathy by identifying with your child's emotions.

Meg used this process when her 4-year-old daughter got upset trying to tie her shoes. When Meg said, "You look really frustrated", the girl launched into an explanation of how she was feeling very frustrated. She then started calming down.

Covering Up Emotions with "I don't care"

During a parenting presentation, a parent asked the school principal "What can I do when my child brings home a test where he did poorly and when I ask him about it he says, 'I don't care'?" The principal responded that whenever she hears a student say, "I don't care", she tries to find the emotions and truth behind those words. She'll ask, "Can you tell me more about that?" The truth may be:

- I'm scared. I need help, but I don't know how to ask for it.

- I'm embarrassed because I don't understand this.

- I feel frustrated because I think this is too hard for me.

Once she understands what the child is communicating, she is in a better position to help. Using empathy and careful listening can help uncover what is really going on.

How is your child feeling when doing this challenging behavior? If you're not sure, ask your child.

Standing Firm Without Arguing

Once you've given your children an answer to a request, using simple responses can help you avoid being pulled into an argument. It can also leave you feeling calmer because you aren't feeling forced to come up with new explanations and reasons for your decision.

Anthony Wolf describes this in <u>The Secret of Parenting</u>. "Perhaps the toughest rule with decision making is that once you decide, you must stand firm. It is a disaster for all when children can regularly wear down their parents and get them to change their minds."[7]

Examples of Simple Responses

Simple phrases work best in response to pleading. For example, if your child wants to play more video games after you've said the time is up and he starts begging you to play longer, you might say:

- "What was my answer?" or
- "I hear you are disappointed."

Once you've made a decision, stick to it without arguing.

Every time he asks you again, you simply repeat the response. If he says something like "That's not fair!" you can respond:

- "Probably not." or
- "I understand you're not happy with stopping."

It's easier to stay calm when you respond the same way every time he comes up with another reason to have more time to play video games.[8]

Avoiding Arguments

What if he tries arguing "Everyone else in my class gets to play video games for at least an hour a day."? You can respond:

- "Regardless …"
- "I understand you're upset."

Avoid defending your position with something like "I don't believe that everyone else in your class even has video games let alone gets to play them an hour each day." By not engaging in a discussion around his objections, you avoid being pulled into an argument.

Could standing firm using a simple response be helpful?

Waiting for Compliance

Sometimes the best option when children do not immediately comply with a request is to repeat the request in a matter-of-fact manner and wait. After repeating your request, do not respond to anything further that they do or say until they have done what you asked.

Patiently Waiting

In <u>The Secret of Parenting</u>, Anthony Wolf, describes a situation where a dad has asked his son to quit banging his fork on the table, but his son didn't stop. Here's the response he recommends:

"Your basic stance as you wait for them to comply should be the same as your attitude while waiting for a bus:

- I am here.
- I am waiting.
- I expect you to stop.
- I am not enjoying the wait.
- I am not going anywhere until you do what I have asked."

Patience is a virtue!

Most kids will comply at which point you can say "thank you".[9]

Learning to Comply with Rules

One of the essential skills any preschooler needs to develop is the ability to follow directions. A preschool director said that all but one of their 70 children had learned to follow directions during the first four months of school. However, Jake refused to follow directions.

For example, one of the school rules is that all children must put on their jackets before going out to play. The kids can take off their jackets and hang them up outside if they are too warm but they need to put them on before they go outside.

Jake frequently refused to put on his jacket. When the teachers discussed the issue with Jake's parents, his dad replied that they don't make Jake do things he doesn't want to do. While it may be easier in the short run to not insist that Jake comply with the rules, in the long run Jake's parents are failing to teach him important social skills.

If you wait patiently, will your child comply with your request?

Teaching Children to Use "I Statements"

Children need to learn how to use words rather than physical force to let someone else know what they want. One way is to teach children to use an "I statement".

The Format of "I Statements"

There are four parts to an "I Statement":

I feel _____ (mad, sad, glad, lonely, scared, ...)

when you _____

because _____

and I want _____.

Starting a statement with "I" instead of "You" is assertive and less likely to make the listener defensive.

Practicing "I Statements"

When children are fighting over something, it is a perfect time for them to use an "I statement".

For example, four-year-old Madison was upset because her five-year-old sister Samantha wouldn't share the paint with her. Madison was about to hit Samantha when her mom decided to intervene and help her learn to use words to let Samantha know how she felt.

Both girls stopped painting while their mom walked them through using "I statements". Madison told her sister "I feel mad when you won't share the red paint with me because I need red for my flower and I want you to share it with me."

Next Samantha repeated back what Madison said to ensure the message was heard. Once she got it correct, it was Samantha's turn. Her statement was "I feel rushed when you keep asking for the red paint because I'm not done with it yet and I want to finish using it."

Madison then repeated back what she heard. Mom then left it up to Madison and Samantha to figure out if they could find a way to share the red paint or if mom needed to put the paint away.

Teach your child "I Statements". Could an "I Statement" be useful in changing your child's challenging behavior?

Telling Children What They Can Do

It's easy to get into the habit of telling children what you don't want them to do instead of what you want them to do. When you want your children to change their behavior, tell them what to do instead of what not to do.

Describing the behavior you do not want:

- "Don't run!"
- "Stop yelling."
- "Don't give me that look!"
- "No throwing cars!"

Make requests without using "no", "don't", "stop"

It's better to say what you do want:

- "Please walk."
- "Please use your soft voice."
- "I'll be happy to talk to you when you are looking at me nicely."
- "You can push the cars on the track."

Telling Kids What They Can Do Using Expectations

While teaching children to share isn't easy, it can help to discuss your expectations for sharing ahead of time.

For example, before other children come over to play you may want to talk to your children about sharing and allow them to select one special toy that can be put away which does not need to be shared. When their friends come over to play, all other toys need to be shared.

These are the established expectations:

- Select one toy to be put away and not shared.
- Share all other toys with friends.

Even after discussing sharing in advance, it is likely for young playmates to get in a fight over a toy. You can then help them figure out how they might be able to share the toy. You will be teaching them an essential friendship skill!

Would telling your child what she can do, instead of what she can't do, reduce her challenging behavior?

Taking "Cool Down" Time

Taking time to cool down can be helpful for children and parents alike! Having a break allows people to regroup and regain their composure. After emotions have cooled, everyone is in a better place for thinking about the situation.

Time-Outs Remove Attention

When children leave a situation for a time-out, they are no longer getting attention. Since behavior that gets attention is likely to be repeated, removing the attention helps.

Time-outs provide breathing room.

Key Points for Making Time-Outs Work

According to the Pediatric Development and Behavior's article "What Makes Time-Out Work (and Fail)?" make sure these items are in place for time-outs to be effective:[10]

- Provide a rich, nurturing "time-in" environment so that the children want to be there.

- When you ask your child to take a time-out, make the request unemotionally, using few words. Do not give lots of warnings before implementing a time-out.

- Do not give children attention while they are in time-out.

- Focus on building self-quieting skills versus a time limit. Allow children to leave time-out once they have quieted themselves and feel they are ready to rejoin the group.

- Use other strategies to teach children new skills. If your child's behavioral problem is due to a lack of skills, teach the missing skills instead of sending him to time-out.

- Be consistent in how time-outs are given.

When your children come back from time-out, be welcoming and avoid giving a lecture about why they were sent to time-out. Children are usually able to figure this out on their own.

Would taking a time-out help reduce your child's challenging behavior?

Establishing Simple Rules

Simple, easy-to-remember rules work well with young children. One way to make sure children understand a rule is to ask them to explain the rule in their own words.

Crying Means Stop

One mom's rule for her 3-year-old and 18-month-old is "Crying means stop." Her kids have learned that if someone is crying then it's time to stop whatever they are doing.

Simple rules work wonderfully for young children.

Both children know the rule and are often able to stop themselves when someone starts crying. However, she does step in if the children are unable to stop themselves or the situation is escalating.

If You Hit, You Sit.

This is a simple rule which lets young children know the consequence of hitting. You can explain that they are welcome to stay if they choose to play cooperatively. You might say, "We want to feel safe when we are together and so if you choose to hit, you must leave."

If children hit:

- Guide them to sitting down nearby (this will probably motivate them to quickly change their behavior to rejoin the fun) or have them go to their room.

- Let children decide when they are ready to return. Tell them they are welcome to come back as soon as they decide to play without hitting.

- Stay calm and avoid showing anger or disappointment. By keeping your emotions under control, children can focus on their own behavior.

- Welcome them back saying something like "I'm happy you've decided to come back. It's more fun when you're with us."

Eventually your children will develop self-control. Until that time, you need to intervene when your children are hitting.

Could a simple rule help with your child's challenging behavior?

Seeking Outside Help

When you notice your child's behavior is continuing and escalating, you know it's time to think of a new approach. If you're struggling to find other options, ask another parent. It's always easier to see solutions to other people's parenting problems rather than your own!

If whatever you have done is not working and you're feeling very discouraged, getting outside help from a parent coach, counselor or child psychologist is a good idea.

What is keeping you up at night?

A mom tearfully described how distant her two children and husband had become. Each one spent most of their time at home in their own worlds of TV, computers, cellphones and video games.

Ignoring problems allows them to grow.

They had even stopped eating supper together. It really bothered her that they were no longer even connecting daily around a meal. They had gotten into a habit of living separately in the same house.

Discussing her feelings with a parent coach gave her the determination to make a change. She decided to begin by holding a family meeting where she would bring up the problem so they could discuss it. She knew changing her family's behavior would probably be a long process and she felt so much better after deciding to take the first step.

When should you look for outside help for your child?

Diane noticed her teenage daughter, Chloe, had been overreacting to little things at home. Diane thought maybe it was from the pressure of school or perhaps just hormones. However, when Chloe blew up at her brother for supposedly losing her hairbands (which in fact Chloe had accidentally tossed in with the dirty laundry), Diane decided to make an appointment for Chloe to see a psychologist.

After seeing Chloe, the psychologist told Diane how serious it was. Chloe had a plan for how she was going to kill herself. Chloe entered an in-patient treatment program and got the help she needed. By paying attention to Chloe's behavior and reaching out for help, Diane may very well have saved Chloe's life. If you feel like something really isn't right within your family, it is wise to get outside help.

Is it time to get additional help for your child's challenging behavior?

Chapter 4: Building Your Kids' Life Skills

If you want your children to launch successfully as adults, there are many skills they need to develop. This chapter looks at how to help your children learn important life skills.

Expressing Emotions in Healthy Ways

Your kids will experience a wide range of emotions each day. They may feel elated one moment followed by disappointment in the next moment.

Perhaps they are thrilled with the red helium balloon they've just been given, only to experience dismay when they forget to hold on and the balloon floats away. Or they may feel terrified in asking someone to the dance and then exhilarated when that person says yes.

Your thoughts trigger your emotions.

Part of being human is experiencing all these different emotions. How your children learn to handle their feelings will affect their success in relationships and school.

Naming Emotions

When your kids are young, they need your help in labeling their feelings. Suppose your child told you he learned at school today that there is a birthday party he's wasn't invited to. If your child is sitting on the couch looking depressed, you might comment "It looks like you are feeling disappointed you didn't get invited to the party." You are helping him feel noticed and teaching a word to attach to his feelings.

Developing a vocabulary for describing feelings gives children words for their emotional experiences. Understanding their own feelings then allows them to appreciate other people's feelings. Correctly reading other people's feelings is essential for building relationships.

These are some words that reflect different emotional intensities:

Abandoned	Empty	Irritated	Panicky
Afraid	Exasperated	Isolated	Rejected
Angry	Excited	Jealous	Shamed
Annoyed	Excluded	Joy	Surprised
Anxious	Frustrated	Judged	Terrified
Criticized	Furious	Lonely	Thrilled
Delighted	Gratitude	Love	Upset
Devastated	Happy	Mistreated	Vulnerable
Disgusted	Horrified	Neglected	Worried
Embarrassed	Humiliated	Overwhelmed	Wounded

You can help your kids develop a range of words to describe mild to strong feelings. Are they furious, angry or feeling slightly bugged? Identifying the feeling's intensity is important in communicating and figuring out what action to take.

Listening to your children's feelings is often the most helpful thing you can do. Talking through big feelings helps kids sort out what's going on. You don't have to fix anything, just listen.

Expressing Unpleasant Emotions

Feelings drive behavior. Part of maturing is being able to respond reflectively rather than reflexively in situations involving strong feelings. Kids need plenty of practice to learn to handle negative feelings well.

While everyone has a right to their feelings, they do not have the right to express those feelings in ways that hurt others. For example, these are some inappropriate expressions of feelings:

- "You're stupid!"
- "You're a mean Mommy!"
- "I hate you!"
- Hitting, biting, shoving, kicking
- Posting mean comments on social media

When your children choose inappropriate behavior, start by acknowledging the feeling you believe is behind the behavior. For example, "You are angry that your brother took your truck, so you hit him." Next suggest a better way to express the emotion, "It's not OK to hit him. You can tell him you are angry and let him know what you want him to do."

Feelings are neither right nor wrong. For example, if teens are feeling rejected by peers, their feelings are valid. Listening to them talk about how they are feeling can help them process those feelings and decide what action to take. How they choose to act on those feelings may or may not be OK.

Trying To Avoid Unpleasant Feelings

Everyone experiences emotional pain; it's part of being human. It's also very human to try to avoid these negative feelings by numbing them. What your kids may not realize is that numbing the painful emotions also numbs the positive ones.

Trying to avoid emotional pain may lead to disastrous results. Some harmful ways kids try to numb emotional pain include things like:

- Drinking, taking drugs
- Cutting themselves
- Seriously restricting food intake
- Injuring someone else or an animal
- Committing suicide

While these actions may temporarily or permanently numb the emotional pain, teaching kids to honestly express their difficult emotions gives them better options. When you allow kids to express their negative feelings, they learn how to talk through their pain rather than try to bury it. Is it easy to listen to someone else's pain? No!

Saying things like "Stop crying!" or "You're not really hurt." teaches kids that expressing emotions like sadness or anger is not OK. However, when children's feelings are validated, they feel understood and recover more quickly. They learn that they can handle difficult feelings and eventually experience relief.

Remember your job is to listen to your children, not to solve their problems. They need to figure out what action to take although you may be able to help them think through consequences of the actions they are considering. Being able to trust you with their most difficult feelings is a life-long gift for your children.

Helping Your Kids Release Emotions Holding Them Back

Emotions start causing problems when they get in your children's way of success. This can happen when they experience something negative and unconsciously decide to make sure that never happens again.

Have you noticed your kids being held back by their emotions? In the following stories, kids are being negatively affected by their strong, persistent feelings.

Brian loved playing baseball and was good at it. One day he was up to bat he got hit hard by the pitcher's ball. He immediately went down in pain but eventually recovered enough to take first base and finish the game. From then on he found various excuses for missing practice and not playing baseball.

Isabel knew she was prepared to take the science test. She had studied all week plus done well on all the homework. However, when she sat down to take the test, her mind went blank.

Mason enjoyed going to school and being with his friends. However, lately he had come to dread being at school. Another boy had decided to start picking on Mason. Every day he had a new way to make Mason feel terrible. Soon Mason was making up excuses about being too sick to go to school but was too ashamed to tell his parents the real reason he didn't want to go to school.

Chris was having fun learning to swim. During one lesson the instructor had the class swim across the pool without touching the wall. Part way through Chris panicked and grabbed the wall. He felt embarrassed as all the other kids made it across the pool without stopping. When it was time to go to the next lesson, Chris refused to get in the car. Eventually his mom cajoled him into getting in the car but when they got to the pool Chris refused to get in water.

Using Tapping To Process Difficult Emotions

All the kids in these stories had emotional forces influencing their behavior. When emotions are at the root of behavior, it doesn't work well to try to use reasoning. For example, trying to reassure a child by saying "You've studied hard. I'm sure you'll do fine on the test." is not likely to help. Nor will it be helpful to tell Chris "Jump in! You're great at swimming."

So if reassuring and reasoning won't work well, what can you do to help your child overcome their fear or anxiety? One thing that has helped both adults and kids is a process called tapping. Tapping combines acknowledging feelings and the reasons behind those feelings along with permission to feel safe and loved in the present moment.

You tap gently on various points in your body while talking through your feelings. While the first time you hear about tapping it may sound ridiculous, it actually has helped lots of people!

Major league athletes use tapping to improve their game performance. Dr. Erin Shannon works with professional baseball and football players both prior to games and during games. To do their best in a game, they use tapping to quickly release any fear of getting hurt or distress from situations at home that are distracting them from the game.[1]

Playing sports is a big part of many kids' lives. To play their best, they need to be emotionally ready. Fear about getting hurt or anxiety about losing can negatively affect a child's performance. Brad Yates has recorded many videos demonstrating using tapping with kids to deal with various difficult feelings. You can watch a video where Yates uses tapping to help a girl prepare to do her best at a soccer game (search YouTube for "Tapping for Kids - Sports - EFT with Brad Yates").[2]

Long term emotional distress gets in the way of living life to the fullest. If your kids are being negatively affected by emotions, tapping may help overcome debilitating emotions. Younger kids usually see tapping as a fun game. They like doing something that makes them feel better. On the other hand, teens are more likely to try tapping if they see it as a type of stress relief – which it definitely is!

What seems to help your kids process their unpleasant feelings?

_____

_____

_____

How could learning about tapping help your kids handle stress better?

_____

_____

_____

Controlling Negative Thoughts

Who will criticize your children the most as they grow up? They will! It is their own negative self-talk that they will hear most often.

Everyone's mind produces a steady stream of thoughts. When these thoughts turn negative then fear, doubt and frustration quickly set in.

Noticing Your Kids' Self-Talk

What your children say provides insight into their thinking. They are engaging in negative self-talk when you hear things like:

- "I'm never going to get this!"
- "Nobody likes me."
- "I can't do it!"

"Your thoughts create your reality -- where you put your focus is the direction you tend to go."
~ Peter McWilliams

Whether your children are struggling with school work, relationships or athletics, their thoughts can help or hinder them.

Dr. Alison Arnold came to my daughter's gymnastics center to work with the kids on the mental side of gymnastics. Athletes need to be in control of their thoughts if they are to give their best performance.

Negative thoughts like these wreak havoc on a gymnast's routine:

- "I'm going to mess up."
- "She's so much better than me."
- "This is too hard for me."

When negative thinking takes over, the likelihood of getting injured increases. You definitely do not want your daughter having negative thoughts right before she does a backhand spring on the beam!

Helping Your Kids Change Their Negative Self-Talk

There is a Zen concept called the Monkey Mind. It's the part of your brain that races from one idea to the next, chattering endlessly, craving things, being unsatisfied and judgmental. Dr. Arnold used this concept to explain negative thinking to the kids. Negative thoughts are like a naughty monkey running away instead of focusing on the task at hand.

What can you do once you notice your Monkey Mind is off in the weeds? You need to flip your negative thinking.

Dr. Arnold discussed a process for flipping negative thinking:

1. Take a deep breath.

2. Think to yourself "Stop. Relax."

3. Say something positive to yourself like "I can handle this." or "I am strong."

By following this process, the kids learned how to stop their negative thoughts and replace them with positive ones.

Paying Attention To Your Own Self-Talk

It's every bit as important to watch out for your own negative thoughts. One of the worst patterns parents can get into is continually thinking about their children's faults.

What you say to your children has a big impact on them. By making more positive comments, you can help them develop more positive self-talk. One way to do this is describe their positive behavior:

- "You sat down, got out your math book and started working on your homework."

- "You shared the crayons with your friend."

- "You waited patiently for your turn to go down the slide."

- "You helped set the table for dinner. I appreciate that."

Your positive comments will help both you and your children focus on what's right instead of what's wrong.

How can you help your children focus on their positive qualities and experiences?

_____

_____

_____

Helping Your Kids Overcome Fear and Anxiety

Feeling anxious isn't fun for anyone. It's natural to want to escape whatever situation is creating the anxiety. However, running away only reinforces the negative feelings associated with it and makes it even harder the next time.

There are also many anxiety producing situations which simply cannot be avoided. For example, everyone must sleep even if going to sleep is difficult due to worries.

Below are some common situations that make children anxious:

- Going to bed, sleeping alone, sleeping with the lights off
- Separating from parents for a play date or being left with another adult
- Encountering animals like dogs, snakes or bugs
- Going to school, taking tests, speaking in front of the class
- Performing in a sport
- Striking up a conversation with a peer, joining in playing
- Being in an enclosed space like an elevator, subway or airplane
- Earthquakes, storms, shootings or other catastrophic events

Handling anxious feelings is an important skill for your kids to develop.

When your children are feeling anxious, it's natural to want to reassure them and make things better. Although some things that you may do can make things worse like:

- Reassuring your child that there is nothing to be afraid of
- Allowing your child to avoid anxiety producing situations
- Performing rituals to reduce your child's anxiety
- Engaging in repetitive discussions around the same anxiety questions
- Having TV news shows on around your children

Let's consider what you can do instead which is more likely to help.

Understanding the Three Parts of Anxiety

In Growing Up Brave[3], Dr. Pincus describes what she calls the "cycle of anxiety". The cycle consists of three components:

What I think

- What if I don't fall asleep tonight?
- I'll probably mess up and the other kids will make fun of me.
- What if mom and dad don't return?

What I do

- Go into mom and dad's room to sleep.
- Skip joining in on the game.
- Plead with mom and dad not to go without me.

What I feel

- My heart starts to beat fast and loud
- My palms get sweaty and my face turns red
- My head and stomach hurt

The cycle can begin with any of the elements – thoughts, actions or feelings. The components work together to keep the cycle going.

Breaking the Cycle of Anxiety

There are several ways to help children overcome their anxiety. One of the ways Pincus explains is to draw a "Bravery Ladder". Each step on the ladder represents one small step towards achieving the overall goal.

For example, if a child is feeling anxious about playing the piano in a recital, the first step might be to play the piano piece at home in front of mom and dad. The next step might be to play the piece in front of a friend. Each step gradually gets the child closer to the goal of being able to play the piece in the recital.

One important aspect is that when children experience the physical symptoms of anxiety like their heart racing or difficulty breathing, they should stay in the situation until these physical responses are reduced by at least half. By hanging in there, the children learn that their bodies will slow down and recover.

It can also be helpful to explore your children's negative thoughts with them. Pincus identifies the two most common types of anxiety thinking involve overestimating the probability of something happening and catastrophizing. For example, a child who is afraid of speaking in front of the class may imagine that he will stand up in front of the class and be totally unable to speak and all the other kids will begin laughing and making fun of him.

You might help your child by asking things like "Have you ever gotten up in front of the class and not been able to say a word? Do other kids feel nervous when they must speak in front of the class? If you see a classmate struggling to speak, do you laugh at them or do you feel like cheering them on? What if kids do laugh, what's the worst thing that will happen to you?"

Exploring questions like these can help your children put their concerns into perspective. Realizing that they can handle other kids laughing, mom and dad probably will make it home safely or that eventually they will fall asleep can help kids control their negative thoughts.

How might a Bravery Ladder help your child overcome a fear?

_____

_____

_____

_____

_____

Setting Healthy Limits

One key skill all kids need to learn is how to set limits for themselves. For children whose parents have always set the limits, leaving home for the first time can be a wild experience. So much freedom, so little experience!

How do children learn to say "no" to themselves? Like everything else, they need practice.

Learning to Set Their Own Limits

When our daughter was in elementary school, she could choose how much dessert to eat after dinner. You'd think that would have brought her great pleasure but in fact it was quite the opposite. She wrestled with just how many pieces of candy she should have and she wanted us to decide - not her!

Being able to set healthy limits will serve your children well throughout their lives.

She would ask us how many pieces she should have. We responded, "Take what you think is a reasonable amount." At which point she demanded back "Well, what is a reasonable amount?" It went on this way night after night. Eventually she developed the ability to decide for herself and set her own limits without checking first with us.

Helping Your Kids Develop Moderation

Messages pour into your children about all the wonderful things they should have - from the latest video games to the best tennis shoes. Do your children need all these things? No, but they certainly want them!

You are left with the challenging task of teaching your children the difference between needs and wants. Learning moderation around spending money and finding out that you can't always have what you want are not easy lessons. It's hard to say "no" to your kids when all the other kids seem to have it. However, if you want your kids to learn moderation, you must be able to say no and stick with it.

When our son was preparing a list of all the things he would need for Junior High, he put a cellphone on the list. This led to a good discussion on the difference between wants and needs. While it was something he wanted, it was definitely nothing he needed.

Setting Healthy Limits Around Sleep

Another area for your kids to practice setting their own limits is around going to bed and getting up. Most kids can handle this sometime during the elementary school years.

How much sleep do your kids need? The National Sleep Foundation has the following sleep recommendations[4]:

- Newborns (0-3 months): 14-17 hours

- Infants (4-11 months): 12-15 hours

- Toddlers (1-2 years): 11-14 hours

- Preschoolers (3-5): 10-13 hours

- School age children (6-13): 9-11 hours

- Teenagers (14-17): 8-10 hours

Sleep experts recommend shutting off all electronic devices at least an hour before bedtime. The light and stimulation interfere with being able to relax and get to sleep.

One mom was complaining about how hard it was to get her teen out of bed in the mornings. When she decided to turn this responsibility over to him, both their lives improved. She stopped nagging him out of bed and he enjoyed feeling competent about getting up himself.

Your children need to learn they are ultimately responsible for setting their own limits. Kids who can set limits for themselves do better in life.

What limits are your children ready to start setting for themselves?

_____

_____

_____

Building Friendship Skills

Are your kids developing the friendship skills they need to succeed? Building and maintaining relationships is essential for your kids' success and happiness.

We all have a deep need for connection with other people. Psychologist Alfred Adler declared that belonging, feeling a sense of connection, is one of the primary motivators of behavior[5]. Your kids are no exception; they too need to feel a sense of belonging.

Are relationship skills easy to learn? No! They take a lot of practice with many different people and situations.

Helping Your Child Develop a Strong Foundation

Your relationship with your child is the foundation on which they will build all other relationships. No matter what your children's age, you can strengthen your relationship by spending time with them.

Your relationship with your children is the foundation for all their other relationships.

Join your children in things they like doing. It might be building with Legos, playing with dolls, playing catch, swinging, biking or jumping on a trampoline. When you participate in activities your children enjoy, you send a strong message about how much you love them and want to be with them. Choose activities that don't involve screens to maximize the interactions you have together.

You may not really like playing with dolls or shooting baskets. That's not the point. You do these activities to be closer to your children. Ideally find activities you both enjoy so you're happy to participate.

Do you always have to be there to play with your children? No! Your children also need to learn to entertain themselves and take responsibility for what to do if they are bored.

Spending Time Together

All kids need lots of time with loving adults and other children to develop their social skills. During a Brain Development & Learning Conference presentation[6], Dr. Bruce Perry explained "There are parts of your brain that are crucial for forming and maintaining relationships - for developing the capacity to be humane, to be empathic, to be capable of sharing, to be capable of self-sacrifice for the people in your family and community. And those parts of the brain develop very much like other parts of the brain in a use-dependent way."

He goes onto explain that like learning a language or physical skill it takes a lot of repetition. Given smaller family sizes, larger classroom sizes and increases in screen time, most kids have significantly less relationship time than previous generations.

What are some signs that your child needs more time interacting with others?

- Your child is not good at sharing with other kids.

- Even when friends come over, your child prefers watching TV or being on a computer to playing with friends.

- Your child struggles to make and keep friends.

- Your child is older than six and does not have at least one close friend.

- Your child likes to be in charge and is reluctant to listen to others.

- Your child acts inappropriately in many social situations.

If you feel your children lack social skills appropriate for their age, they need more opportunities for practice. They may prefer being alone or playing on their digital devices, however, those activities do not build social skills. It's only by participating in relationships that your children learn the intricacies of making them work.

Threatening to Remove Connection

When children want to hurt others, one of the primary ways they do it is by threatening to remove connection. Even young children know the power of saying things like:

- "I'm not your friend anymore"

- "I don't want to play with you."

- "You're not invited to my birthday party!"

- "Go away and leave me alone!"

Words can really hurt. Children need help learning to express their feelings in healthier ways than threatening to no longer be friends.

Helping Your Child Practice Friendship Skills

After attending my presentation at his son's elementary school, a dad wrote me about his 10-year-old son's struggle to make friends. "While the kids play together, he has not made any fast friends yet. We thought that this would change when we moved to this new school but I have not seen any progress. Rather, his experience in school is not great and he is constantly targeted by the popular kids and often shunned by them when he tries to mingle."

His son was increasingly satisfied just to stay home playing his XBOX instead of being with friends. This dad decided to try a number of ideas to help his son build his friendships:

- Planned an outing to a swimming pool and allowed his son to choose someone to invite along.

- Invited a friend over to their house for a couple hours to help build a fort.

- Started attending a YMCA family night where his son met new friends.

- Encouraged his son to join the school band where he also made friends who shared his interest in music.

When your children are young, you will be involved in speaking to the other parents to arrange activities. As your children get older, it's important that they reach out initially to their friends about getting together. You can follow-up with the parents to finalize the details.

It will take time for your children to discover their real friends and even these relationships will undoubtedly run into a few twists, turns and potholes along the way. However, developing strong friendships is worth the effort. Having good friends where your children can be their authentic selves is a key ingredient to their happiness.

Understanding Friendship Rules

One of the most heartbreaking things is to see your child struggling to make and keep friends. Your child might be shy, overly sensitive, intimidating or the vulnerable child who is continually being picked on.

What can you do to help your child develop the skills needed to make good friends?

Many of the rules of friendship are unwritten. Some kids easily catch on to those rules while others struggle.

In their book The Unwritten Rules of Friendship: Simple Strategies to Help Your Child Make Friends[7], Elman and Kennedy-Moore define the characteristics of 10 types of children who often have problems with friendships. They describe the behaviors that these kids exhibit that turn their peers off. They then list the missing unwritten friendship rules and how you can help your child develop those skills.

Some of the unwritten rules include things like:

- There is no such thing as a perfect friend.
- If you hit someone, odds are they'll hit you back harder.
- Dwelling on bad feelings makes them worse.
- When someone says "Stop", stop.
- Staying out of harm's way is wise.
- You don't have to stay around people who are unkind to you.

If your child is struggling with friends, helping your child figure out these unwritten rules can be extremely helpful.

Finding Good Friends

One of the most complex tasks of growing up is figuring out how to fit into the peer group. If your child struggles to fit in, it can be agonizing for both you and your child. You would like to protect your child and yet you really have limited abilities within your child's peer group.

Is there any way you can help? Mary was concerned about how her grade school daughter, Samantha, was struggling to find friends at her new school. Mary decided to try to help by asking Samantha who she thought might be a good friend and why. After she identified three girls, Mary helped Samantha invite each girl over for either a play date or to go somewhere fun. Spending one-on-one time with each girl helped Samantha grow closer to those girls.

Mary also thought it would help Samantha to have a group of friends outside of school. Since Samantha had shown an interest in dancing, Mary helped her find a dancing class where she met a few girls who had similar interests. It was a slow process but eventually Samantha started making a few good friends.

Differences Between Belonging and Fitting In

The terms "belonging" and "fitting in" are sometimes used interchangeably. However, they are very different concepts.

In Brené Brown's book The Gifts of Imperfection she states, "One of the biggest surprises in this research was learning that fitting in and belonging are not the same thing, and, in fact, fitting in gets in the way of belonging. Fitting in is about assessing a situation and becoming who you need to be to be accepted. Belonging, on the other hand, doesn't require us to change who we are; it requires is to be who we are."[8]

The best gift you can give your children is a strong sense of love and belonging within your family. When you love and appreciate your children for who they are, they can be authentic. Children shouldn't have to fake it to belong at home.

What relationship skills do you feel your children need to work on?

_____

_____

_____

What activities might help your children build their friendship skills?

_____

_____

_____

Developing Habits to Succeed in School

Can developing good habits help your kids succeed in school? Yes! Habits are powerful patterns of behavior that automatically unfold in certain situations. By establishing helpful habits, your kids will have routines that help them succeed in school.

The brain loves to establish habits because it takes less thinking and energy. For example, when your children are learning something like how to tie their shoes, it will take all their focus to accomplish the task. Once they master it, their brains will use far less energy as the process becomes automatic.

Good habits make school easier!

Given how powerful habits are, it is worth figuring out which ones will help your kids succeed in school.

Looking at How Habits Form

In The Power of Habit: Why We Do What We Do in Life and Business, Charles Duhigg describes a three-step process he calls the habit loop:

"First, there is a cue, a trigger that tells your brain to go into automatic mode and which habit to use. Then there is the routine, which can be physical or mental or emotional. Finally, there is a reward, which helps your brain figure out if this particular loop is worth remembering for the future.

Over time, this loop - cue, routine, reward; cue, routine, reward - becomes more and more automatic. ... When a habit emerges, the brain stops fully participating in decision making. It stops working so hard, or diverts focus to other tasks. So unless you deliberately fight a habit - unless you find a new routine - the pattern will unfold automatically." [9]

There are many things that can serve as a cue for your kids' habits:

- Hearing the alarm going off in the morning.
- Walking into the kitchen.
- Stopping in the bathroom.
- Entering the house right after coming home from school.
- Sitting down at a desk to do homework.

Any of these cues can launch a habit. Upon hearing the alarm go off, your children might have the habit of hitting the snooze button or they might have the habit of doing some stretches before getting out of bed. If they're in the habit of hitting the snooze button, they are probably able to do this without really thinking - a bit risky!

Establishing Healthy Habits that Lead to School Success

By developing healthy habits for common routines, your kids will be setting themselves up for success.

Morning routine -

- What time do your kids need to get up to not feel rushed?
- What do they need to get done before leaving for school?
- What healthy breakfast food would they like to have available? By the time most kids are in grade school, they can be responsible for making their own breakfast.

Free morning charts and bedtime charts are available to print here: PricelessParenting.com/Chart-for-Kids

After school routine -

- What healthy snacks would they like to have after school?
- What type of exercise would they like to do?
- Where do they want to do their homework? Will they have music playing? Will they have their cell phones on?
- How much electronic entertainment time are they allowed?
- When will chores be done?

Evening routine -

- What do they need to have done before going to bed? Will they be packing their backpack or lunch for the next day?
- When do electronics get turned off for the day and where are they stored? Kids who sleep with their cell phones, computers and video games in their rooms have more sleep disturbances.
- What time do they need to turn out the lights to get enough sleep?

Answering these questions can help your kids figure out habits that will help them succeed.

Taking Responsibility

Whose responsibility is it that your children remember their homework, books, lunch and other supplies? It's your kid's responsibility! Many parents are tempted to make this their responsibility instead of their children's.

One mom was fed up with reminding her 5th grade son to bring his soccer equipment to school. He often responded in an irritated tone, "I know Mom, I know!" One day she decided to stop reminding him.

That night she did mention to him that he might want to put his soccer supplies by his backpack to remind himself to take it in the morning. He decided not to follow her advice and left the next morning without his soccer equipment. When he got home from school that day he was upset he had to practice without his equipment. However, that was the last time he forgot!

By turning responsibility over to your children, they learn to be capable and competent. You may need to teach your kids some skills so they can independently handle their morning, afternoon and evening routines. Focus on helping them learn these new skills and resist the urge to jump in and do it for them.

What habits could help your kids experience more success?

_____

_____

_____

_____

_____

Persevering Through Challenges

One of the hardest parts about being a parent is watching your children struggle. Whether your child is struggling to master a new skill in a sport or a homework assignment, it can be hard to take a step back and let your child handle it.

There's a Native American legend of a man watching a butterfly as it fought to emerge from a small hole in its cocoon. He watched for several hours as the butterfly struggled to force its body through this little hole. After a while it stopped pushing and seemed to have given up. The man decided to help the butterfly by carefully enlarging the hole. The butterfly quickly emerged but its body was swollen and its wings were shriveled. It crawled around dragging its wings.

Struggling is often required to get through difficult situations.

What the man didn't realize was that the butterfly needed to struggle through the small opening to force the fluids from its body into its wings which would strengthen them to fly. Having missed that opportunity to push through the small opening, the butterfly was weak and was never able to fly.

The man's desire to help that butterfly sadly had the opposite effect. Children are a lot like butterflies. They need to struggle to learn how to fly.

Doing Your Own Work

Children learn by doing. When your children do a task, they build their brain connections. When you do a task for them, you reinforce your own brain connections without adding to theirs.

Do your children ever complain about not being able to do something? My daughter complained that she wasn't good at making peanut butter sandwiches so she wanted me to do it for her. I responded that this was the exact reason she needed to practice doing it! If I kept making the sandwiches for her, she'd never learn how to do it herself.

Did she thank me for this opportunity to practice? No. However, eventually she did get very good at making peanut butter sandwiches!

During my son's 4th grade curriculum night the teacher announced she would not be giving much homework. One mom excitedly responded how happy she was to hear this! She mentioned that there were several nights last year that her daughter would go to bed and she would be up until midnight finishing her daughter's projects.

When other parents in the room expressed surprise, she explained that her daughter needed her rest and certainly couldn't be staying up that late doing homework. What do you think her daughter learned from this? How did she feel when her mother finished her homework?

Practicing Perseverance

My son took Taekwondo for many years starting at age seven. Along with the rest of the kids, he memorized the tenets of Taekwondo: courtesy, integrity, perseverance, self-control and indomitable spirit. Developing these qualities was essential as he worked towards achieving his second-degree black belt.

The hardest part for me was watching him struggle to break a board during testing. Clearly, I couldn't jump in and do it for him. All I could do was silently cheer him on from the sidelines. He had to find it within himself to try again and again until he broke the board.

His instructor, Master Shin, told the kids that breaking a board was a lot like achieving any other goal in life. To reach the goal, you must focus on it and exert the right amount of energy at just the right time. You must not stop when your fist or foot touches the board but rather go through the board. By following this advice and persevering, my son broke many boards.

What struggles are your children currently facing?

_____

_____

_____

What are your children learning from their efforts to overcome these difficulties?

_____

_____

Learning through Chores

You have until your children are about 18-years-old to teach them all the basic skills they'll need to live on their own. That's a lot of teaching! Doing household chores is a great way for kids to learn those skills.

It's also important for children to learn that being part of a family means helping with household tasks. You do not want your children growing up seeing you as their personal servant!

Starting Chores Early

Start chores when your children are young and enthusiastic. Although preschoolers are not very good at chores, they are often eager to help. When you give your preschoolers simple chores, they are on the road to being significant contributors to your family.

Chore chart and chore ideas are available here: PricelessParenting.com/Chart-for-Kids

Young children can handle tasks like picking up their toys, bringing in the mail and putting napkins and silverware on the table. You will need to teach your children how to do each task and help them out until they can do it on their own.

One mom said she is teaching her 5-year-old twins how to do the laundry. Although she still needs to provide some guidance, the boys are so proud they know what buttons to push and how to do a load of laundry!

Mastering new household skills builds self-confidence in children. It also builds appreciation for what needs to be done to keep the household running.

When my son was in elementary school one of his chores was washing the kitchen floor. We typically take our shoes off in the house but one day I kept my shoes on while carrying in some groceries. He asked me to take my shoes off because he had just finished cleaning the floor. Now that was music to my ears!

Choosing Chores

Begin by writing down all the tasks that need to be done to keep your family going. Include things like going to work to earn money, paying bills and providing rides.

Next, sit down with your kids to discuss how to divide up these tasks. You may want to sign up for all the tasks that you need to do like pay the internet bill. Once they see how many tasks you are doing for the family, they'll be primed to take on their fair share.

Some families choose to have daily chores to cover all the household tasks. Other families save larger tasks for the weekend. They might divvy up those tasks by letting kids choose slips of paper with tasks from a hat.

Whichever way you decide to handle chores, it's important for each person to understand their chores and when they need to be done. You may want to post a chore list in the kitchen or some other public area.

Tracking Completed Chores

It is your children's responsibility to remember to do their chores. How will they keep track of when their chores are done? They may want to have a chore chart where they check off their chores once they are completed. Another approach is to have a calendar where they write their initials once their chores are done.

Some parents have their kids tell them when they are done with their chores. The parents may check to make sure the chores were done well. Some change the Wi-Fi password daily and give it to their kids after the chores are completed.

What if your child wants to postpone a chore? You may want to allow your kids to do two chores the following day. Be careful not to allow postponing multiple days of chores or it will become too difficult for them to make up.

You may decide to help your child out with a chore occasionally. You'll know they appreciate it if they thank you for helping them out. You may also decide to allow your child to skip chores on special occasions.

Paying for Extra Chores

One way to allow your children to earn money is to pay them for doing extra chores in addition to their normal ones. It's a great way to get work done and for your children to earn money for special things.

One summer our then 12-year-old son learned to pressure wash the deck. He was happy to take on this new task especially since it involved getting wet and getting paid! My husband taught him how to use the pressure washer including all the safety information. It took many hours to get the job done but he stuck with it and we enjoyed a clean deck.

Your kids can also use extra chores to earn something they want. Our children earned a trampoline by each doing 100 extra chores. It took them almost a year to accomplish this. They were proud when they finished earning the trampoline!

Doing chores are a part of life. When you expect your kids to help around the house, it builds their competence and sense of responsibility. These are skills which will help them out in school and later in life.

How do your children indicate when they've completed their chores?

_____

_____

_____

What happens if the chores aren't done?

_____

_____

_____

Teaching Financial Responsibility

Providing an allowance is a wonderful way to begin teaching your children about money. It is also a great way to give them some control over spending decisions and avoid arguments in the store!

Starting an Allowance

It may seem counterintuitive to give your child an allowance to save money but it works! Anything extra your children would like at the store can now be their responsibility to purchase. When they ask to buy something, you can say "Sure, as long as you have enough money."

Children think longer and harder when spending their own money rather than their parents' money.

By the time children are 4-years-old, most are ready for a small allowance. Having their own money helps children learn about the value of money. They learn important skills like saving up for a special purchase.

Some parents help their children put their money into three different containers – one for spending, one for saving and one for donating. By dividing up their allowance into these areas, kids start learning about saving up for the future and also helping others out through donations.

Do not tie your children's allowance to their chores. Chores are done as part of being in the family whether or not your children want an allowance that week. Parents who tie allowance and chores together often find that their kids refuse to help around the house unless there is money involved.

Allowing Kids to Make Spending Mistakes

Marcus told the story of how he was shopping with his 6-year-old son and his son decided he really wanted to buy a toy car. The car he wanted was flimsy and the dad was fairly sure that it wouldn't last long before it broke. Marcus mentioned his concerns to his son but still allowed his son to make his own choice on whether or not to buy it.

Well his son bought the car. Within a week of having it, the front wheels broke off. Instead of saying "I told you so", Marcus helped his son glue it back together. Although it wasn't quite as good as before, the son thanked his dad for helping him fix it. This boy's respect for his dad grew along with some wisdom about buying cheap toys.

Opening Bank Accounts and Learning About Credit

It's helpful to get a bank account started when children are young so they can begin saving for their future. When they are older, you can help them get checkbooks, learn about keeping track of their account balances and learn about credit. It is especially important to discuss credit cards and interest payments.

One dad was shocked to learn his 25-year-old daughter didn't realize that when she made the minimum credit card payment she was going to be charged a steep interest rate on the remaining balance. She quickly learned this point when she saw her next credit card statement!

How do you handle allowance for your children?

_____

_____

_____

_____

What things are your children responsible for purchasing for themselves?

_____

_____

_____

_____

Following Important Rules

You establish rules to help keep your kids safe. When faced with tough decisions, your rules can guide your children to making good choices.

Unthinkingly Breaking Rules

NBC's Dateline tested a few kids in tough situations in a program called "The Perils of Parenting". They set up various situations where the kids were recorded on hidden cameras. Parents were interviewed ahead of time and asked how they thought their children would respond. Parents expressed how they hoped their children would act but often had nagging doubts as to how their kids would behave.

Only set rules that you truly care enough about to enforce.

In one scenario, 12 and 14-year-old siblings were home alone when a man with a badge knocked on their door. Much to their parents' disappointment, they opened the door and let him in when he explained that he was in the neighborhood inspecting milk. This scenario had been used successfully by a real child predator.

Explaining Rules To Your Kids

Does the way you word a rule matter? Yes! How you state a rule can greatly affect your children's ability to follow the intention of the rule. For example, there are different ways you might state the rule about not opening the door:

- "Don't open the door to strangers." For this rule, your children need to first establish if they feel the person at the door is a stranger. This may be a more difficult judgment if the person appears to be a police officer or some other official.

- "Don't open the door to anyone when you are home alone." Does this rule still apply if there are multiple children at home but no parent is home?

- "Don't open the door to anyone if a parent isn't around." Is it OK to open the door if a parent is home but asleep?

- "Only parents open the door when someone knocks." This may be the easiest rule to follow especially for young children.

You want to state rules in ways that are easy for your kids to follow.

Helping Kids Think Through The Rules

It can help to discuss "what if" scenarios. For example, if the rule is don't approach a stranger's car, talk through possibilities like these:

- What if the driver says he has a question he wants to ask you? Do you go closer to the car so you can hear the question?

- What if the lady driving says her puppy is lost and she needs your help finding it? She has a picture of the puppy that she wants to give you. Do you go get the picture?

- What if the man driving holds up a gift and says it's for you. Do you go to the car to get the gift?

Discussing these scenarios helps your kids consider different aspects of the rules. Your kids will be better prepared to follow the intent of the rules when they've tried out the rules in pretend situations.

Testing The Rules

Sometimes your kids may not appreciate why you have certain rules. They may test the rules and learn through the consequences.

One family developed many rules around the use of the internet like never giving away your real name, phone number or email address. A related rule was to never use "stranger hook-up" websites.

13-year-old Rachel knew these rules well. However, when a friend excitedly told her about a website where they could meet boys, Rachel was eager to try it out. They met boys from all over the country! These boys made Rachel feel wonderful with all their compliments, so she decided to give them her name, number and email address.

Rachel experienced some serious consequences when these "boys" started hounding her through cellphone and email. When one showed up in Seattle and wanted to get together, the police became involved.

Her parents decided to help Rachel by limiting these types of choices for a while. When she's more prepared to handle her cellphone and computer responsibly, she'll have another chance.

Reducing Rules By Providing Reasons

Have you ever told your kids not to touch something only to have them immediately try touching it? Being told not to do something naturally makes kids curious about what will happen if they do it.

If you were walking in a park on a warm summer day near a sparkling stream, would you or your kids be tempted to cool off in the stream? Splashing around in some cool water on a hot day feels great!

What if there was a sign nearby saying, "Stay Out Of The Creek"? Would that make you stay on the path or would you feel even more drawn to the water? Simply being told not to do something can make the forbidden even more tempting. You can probably come up with many justifications for ignoring the sign and going into the creek. Perhaps you will go a little way downstream from the sign so as not to break the rules right in front of the sign!

Providing Two Good Reasons

A neighborhood Seattle park has a beautiful creek flowing through it. There is a bridge over the creek and a dirt area near one side of the bridge which provides easy access to the creek.

Instead of telling people to stay out of the creek, the park service put up a sign providing valuable information about the creek. The sign's title is "Two Reasons to Stay Out of this Creek".

The first reason listed is bacteria; "Urban creeks contain bacteria that can make people and dogs sick." It explains how bacteria gets into the creek and what you can do to reduce the bacteria in the creek. Excellent points … the last thing you want is to be sick!

The second reason listed is wildlife; "This creek is home to fish, insects, birds and other wildlife. Staying out of the creek will help keep their home or habitat in good condition." This appeals to your desire to help protect the environment.

Reasons That Work Well

How could giving reasons apply to parenting situations? It's more powerful to explain possible consequences of choices to your kids rather than to tell them what to do.

For example, instead of telling your kids not to use drugs, tell them what is likely to happen to their brains and bodies if they use drugs. My kids were horrified when they saw pictures of people who had been doing meth for a couple years. Their teeth were black and rotten. Their faces were sunken with sores all over. This left a huge impression on them!

You could also explain how a choice to use drugs may affect others. Kids who use drugs need money to buy drugs and often turn to stealing to get that money. Family members may no longer feel comfortable having those kids over to their house due to having things stolen. Whenever possible use real stories to highlight the consequences of choices. You can use stories from family and friends or news stories.

Another example is when you take young kids to the store. Instead of telling them to stay right by you explain why keeping close to you is in their best interest. You might mention that they will feel scared if they can't find you and that you would feel worried too.

It would also be good to tell them what to do in the unfortunate case that you do get separated. Teach your kids how to identify safe adults to ask for help. Asking for help from a mom who has kids is a fairly safe option.

Making Your Job Easier

You might think that you should not have to explain your reasoning to your kids. If you give them an order, then they should obey – no questions asked. However, when you give your kids orders and rules, you are doing the thinking instead of them. What happens when you are not around to give the orders or ensure the rules are followed?

Help your kids consider the consequences of their choices. This information will empower them to make wise choices not simply obey rules. When you can count on your kids making wise decisions on their own, your parenting job is so much easier!

Look at the rules you have for your kids. Which rules are necessary and which ones can be replaced by giving your kids reasons so they can do their own thinking?

_____

_____

Building Kids' Confidence Through Creativity

What creative activities do your kids like? When they have unscheduled time and aren't on their digital devices or watching TV, what do they like to do?

Are they the artistic type who likes to draw, paint or make sculptures out blocks or rocks? Do they enjoy making up new dance moves or their own music? Are they drawn to acting out make believe stories or creating plays with other kids? Do they love being outside designing obstacle courses or challenging jumps for trying out on their skateboards? Do they like baking or cooking?

Creativity needs time and space to grow.

Part of growing up is figuring out what you like to do and what you're good at. When your kids find a passion and devote time to it, they build their confidence with their accomplishments. Trying out various creative activities will help them discover their gifts and talents.

Making Space For Creativity

Creativity can't be rushed. Have you ever noticed that you'll figure out a problem or have a new idea when you are relaxing and not even thinking about it? Perhaps your best ideas come to you first thing in the morning or while you are showering.

Your kids need down time to tap into their creativity. This means time without being entertained by digital devices or other activities. Daydreaming and even being bored are prerequisites for creativity!

Some kids are so accustomed to being constantly entertained that they quickly complain about being bored. If this sounds familiar, have your kids write down activities that they like doing on slips of paper. These should be activities which don't involve digital technology. Put these slips of paper into a container. When they are bored, have them pick two slips out and choose one of those activities.

Engaging In The Creative Process

Before you can create something, you need an inspiration for what it is you want to create. If your children do not know what they want to create, then it's time for daydreaming and imagining new possibilities.

Once your kids have their idea, they are ready to begin! Creating something is a process that involves three steps:

1. Setting an intention on what you want to create

2. Figuring out what needs to happen to bring about your intention

3. Taking action to bring your intention into reality

The creative process is rarely smooth. Your children will likely have to deal with unanticipated problems and things not working out as well as they had imagined. This is not failure rather it is creativity's iterative nature. Your kids will be learning how to adjust when things do not go as planned.

Creativity works best when kids feel they can start over, they are not rushed and there's no grading or judging. Being creative should feel expansive, not restrictive.

When your kids finally achieve their intention, they can be proud! Their accomplishments will leave them feeling more confident and capable.

Discovering Passions Through Creativity

Going through the creative process helps your kids listen to their inner voice. They'll be discovering what they like to do and where their talents lie. They'll start getting ideas about how they can contribute to creating a better world.

Before your kids can be happy, they need to know what makes them feel alive and engaged. Too many teenagers report feeling like they're living someone else's life. They've spent their time following other people's directions. They feel lost and uninspired.

Giving your kids opportunities to be creative helps them spend time listening to themselves. Ideally your kids will build their lives around their passions. When your kids know what makes their hearts' sing, they are on their way to creating the life of their dreams.

What creative activities do your kids enjoy?

_____

_____

Chapter 5: Leading with Your Best Parenting

Priceless® Parenting

You are the leader in your family. When you have the support and skills to do your best parenting, you will be the parent you want to be.

Striving To Do Your Best

Are you striving to be an excellent parent? Of course you want to be an excellent parent! You love your kids and want to do the best for them. You may read parenting articles, books and take classes. You're working hard to raise your children well.

Judging Yourself

How do you measure how you are doing? If you were grading yourself as a parent, what grade would you give yourself? Do you score 100%? 110%? 60%?

Do not compare yourself to other parents.

What is the cut off for excellent parenting? Do you need to score at least 95%?

If these questions seem reasonable, you probably spent many years in schools that graded your work. You know what it's like to strive for the perfect score. You know how it feels to get the top score and how it feels to fall short.

The problem is relationships defy measurement. Nobody is giving out extra credit for getting your kids into bed on time or making a meal together. No psychologist will be assessing how well you've prepared your kids to launch as young adults.

Searching for the Right Answers

When you take tests in school, there are right answers and wrong answers. If you want to get a top score, you must know the right answers.

Finding the right answers involves judging different choices. What are the right answers in parenting? The decisions you need to make start off right from the beginning.

- Breast feed or bottle feed?
- Circumcise or not?
- Sleep with you or sleep in the crib?
- Cloth diapers or paper diapers?

You may have strong feelings about your decisions and perhaps have been involved in heated discussions over the pros and cons of various choices. Wanting to believe that you've made the right decision leads to judging other parents' choices. However, there are very few clear-cut right or wrong decisions and plenty of gray areas.

Trying to be the Perfect Parent

When striving for excellence it's easy to slip into desiring perfection. You may not even realize you've transitioned from healthy striving to wanting perfection. What does it look like if you are trying to be a perfect parent?

- You are hard on yourself. You can see many ways you could do better. The little voice in your head is often critical.

- You are hard on your kids. You believe their success in school, music and sports is a direct reflection on you as a parent. You need them to do well to validate your competence as a parent.

- Your kids need to look good. You certainly do not want your preschooler going to school in mismatched clothes she chose herself because it would reflect poorly on you.

- You find yourself critiquing your partner's parenting. Your partner complains about you micromanaging and second guessing.

- Sometimes you feel frozen in responding to your children's behavior. You don't want to do the wrong thing. What is the right thing to do in this situation? Is there an app you can check?

- You are afraid of messing your children up. You're worried that your parenting will send them into counseling later on.

That's a lot of pressure. It's hard to enjoy your family or have fun together with the stress of trying to get it right.

In her book <u>The Gifts of Imperfection</u> Brené Brown discusses healthy striving versus perfectionism. "Understanding the difference between healthy striving and perfectionism is critical to laying down the shield and picking up your life. Research shows that perfectionism hampers success. In fact, it's often the path to depression, anxiety, addiction, and life paralysis."[1]

Certainly you do not want to be taking the path to depression, anxiety and addiction! Parenting is hard enough without trying to measure yourself against impossible goals.

Instead, take a deep breath and appreciate that you are trying your best. Remind yourself that what your kids need is good enough parenting, not perfect parenting.

Practicing Stress Reducing Self-Care

Do you find yourself feeling guilty when you think about taking time for yourself? If you're a parent, there are a million other things that need to be done - laundry, dishes, helping with homework, making dinner, driving the kids around and the list goes on.

Do you feel like there isn't enough time to get all the things you'd like to have done each day? Is your schedule crammed full? Does adding your own self-care to that list make it feel even more overwhelming?

Taking care of yourself is always important and it's even more critical if you are feeling overwhelmed. Nobody will do it for you – in fact others are likely to encourage you to put even more on your plate that has nothing to do with taking care of yourself!

Defining Your Own Self-Care

Renée Trudeau, author of <u>Nurturing the Soul of Your Family</u>, defines self-care as "the art of attuning and responding to your deepest needs and desires"[2]. If you have focused on attending to others for many years, it can be hard to tune into your own needs. It may even seem foreign to consider your needs and desires.

What does self-care look like to you? Moment to moment you may have different answers. Self-care may be:

- Singing, dancing, doing yoga

- Biking, hiking, swimming, going for a run

- Playing the piano, strumming the guitar, tapping on drums

- Taking a nap

- Saying "no" to a request

- Saying "I need to think about that. I'll get back to you."

- Meditating, praying
- Painting, drawing, sewing, knitting, wood carving
- Gardening, cooking, baking
- Taking a hot bath or a cold shower

You are the one who knows your needs and desires. It's up to you to reflect on what you most need and prioritize getting your needs met.

Prioritizing Taking Care of Yourself

You can neglect your self-care for a while, maybe even years. Eventually it catches up with you in the form of discontent, depression, disease or an uneasy feeling that there must be more to life.

Tragically some parents end up at this point and become suicidal. A mother of three wonderful kids found herself feeling increasingly depressed. Although her children were all excelling in school and other activities, she just wasn't satisfied ... not with them and not with herself.

She eventually got to such a low point that she turned to professionals for help. After a year of hard work, she rebalanced herself and overcame her depression. Much of what she had to do was start putting herself first. She had to figure out what activities she wanted to pursue ... not for her family but for herself.

One thing she loved to do was to sing. While she drove her kids around to their choir practices, she no longer was singing in a group herself. So she joined a choir and added the joy of singing back to her life. Each step took time; it wasn't easy but it paid off.

A boy at the school where my husband teaches wasn't as fortunate. Tragically his mother committed suicide and left the family struggling to cope. It's extremely difficult for any child to handle a parent's death and even more challenging when that death is a suicide.

Taking care of yourself is essential because your family needs you. You are irreplaceable to your children. One of the best gifts you can give them is being fully present for them. You can only do this if you take care of yourself.

Figuring Out What You Need Most

A place deep within you knows what you need. It's hard to hear your own wise inner voice with the TV or computer on. You really need to quiet down and slow down.

This is easier said than done! If all you can carve out is five minutes of quiet time, start with that. Just get comfortable being quietly by yourself. Focusing on your breathing is one way to quiet down your mind. Various meditation practices can be helpful in learning to still your thoughts.

By taking time to quiet down, you will be able to hear the wisdom within you. There is a part of you that knows what you most need and desire. If you slow down and listen, you will find your answers. It's a gift to both yourself and your family.

What is it you need most right now?

_____

_____

_____

_____

What do you need to do to prioritize taking care of yourself?

_____

_____

_____

_____

Setting Healthy Boundaries Within Your Family

Healthy boundaries are essential to living together harmoniously as a family. Good boundaries are like fences defining the edges of what is acceptable and unacceptable. Being sensitive to everyone's boundaries is essential for smooth sailing.

How do you know when you've crossed a boundary? If you are paying attention to the other person's reaction, they'll often let you know. For example, children being tickled may be laughing but then it becomes too much and they say "stop". They've gone from feeling comfortable to uncomfortable. When you stop tickling, you honor their boundary.

Honoring personal boundaries shows respect.

Noticing Personal Boundaries

Before you can honor someone's boundaries, you must notice them. Megan realized her son Alex was sensitive to various scents when he started complaining about smells. The smell of the laundry detergent bothered Alex so they switched to unscented laundry detergent and dryer sheets. Megan stopped wearing perfume or using hair spray - all way too smelly! She also changed to using unscented candles.

While the rest of the family was fine with these scents, Alex's boundary for acceptable smells was much narrower. All these little adjustments helped Alex stay in his comfortable zone.

Different people have different boundaries and tolerances for stretching those boundaries. One mom realized their family's schedule felt too crazy when the kids had more than one extracurricular activity at a time. They decided to limit their kids to one activity at a time.

In the spring their son wanted to join both baseball and the school play which overlapped by a couple weeks. They carefully considered the impact this would have and decided that although it crossed the boundary it would be doable. Other families may have decided it would have stretched them too thin.

Recognizing a Boundary Breach

How does it feel when your boundaries are crossed? Depending on the situation, you may experience feelings like:

- Anger – if you believe someone has intentionally crossed a boundary

- Resentment – if you've tried to say no but reluctantly agreed

- Overwhelm – if you're taking on too much

- Regret – if you wish you would have defended your boundary but instead you caved in

How do you respond once you realize a boundary has been crossed? You might …

- Ignore that the boundary has been crossed

- Respond reflexively by doing something like yelling in anger

- Respectfully address the boundary issue

The last option is the best for fixing the boundary breach while also maintaining loving relationships.

Respectfully Responding To Boundary Breaches

Noticing when a boundary is being stretched gives you the best chance to respond in a calm, respectful way. By speaking up immediately, you take responsibility for your own needs. You'll have a better chance to respond respectfully before the boundary is broken and you've reached the "I can't take it anymore" point.

When you set a boundary, you are declaring a limit. Others may respect your boundary or they may test it. Kids test boundaries by begging, whining or simply doing what they know they are not supposed to do. When that happens how do you respond?

Before acting, you may want to put a hand on your heart and take a few deep breaths. This breath break will help you center yourself. Feeling more grounded will allow you to act from your higher self.

Now you are ready to re-establish your boundary. It might sound like this:

Situation: Your child is jumping on the couch even though you've told them not to.

Establishing boundary: You lift your child off the couch and onto the floor. You tell them they can jump as much as they want on the floor.

Situation: Your family has been invited over for dinner at your aunt's house. Although you appreciate the offer, your week has been crazy so you politely decline the invitation. Your aunt pleads with you to come arguing that you need to eat so you might as well come over.

Establishing boundary: You repeat your boundary saying something like "I appreciate the invitation and it's not going to work for us this weekend."

Situation: Your child wants to go over to a friend's house. After asking a few questions you realize the friend's parents are not home and so you tell your child no. Your child begs you to change your mind adding that other kids are going, and their parents are letting them.

Establishing boundary: You stick with your answer saying "Regardless, I am not comfortable with you going."

Situation: You are waiting in line to get into an event at your kids' school. Someone cuts in front of you.

Establishing boundary: You say to that person, "Pardon me. We've been waiting for a while in this line and the back of the line is actually over there."

Maintaining your boundaries means having your own back. You respectfully stand up for yourself. By standing up for yourself, you teach people what you will and will not tolerate.

Plan on stating your boundary many times using similar words. Other people will often push back and express their disappointment. Take another deep breath and restate your position.

Setting and maintaining boundaries is a skill your kids will use for the rest of their lives. When you model maintaining healthy boundaries, your kids learn how to do this.

Where do you want to set better boundaries?

_____

_____

Understanding Men and Women React Differently to Stress

How often does parenting leave you feeling stressed? When you care about how something will turn out, there is a certain amount of stress involved. One of the things you care most about is your children.

Whether it's getting your kids to school on time, coordinating schedules or dealing with misbehavior, raising kids involves stress. Gender differences between men and women affect how each respond to that stress. Understanding these differences and providing the support your partner needs can make the difference between a relationship that grows and one that falls apart.

Additional Stress from Children

Dr. John Medina describes the additional stress babies bring in his book Brain Rules for Baby. "For most first-time moms and dads, the first shock is the overwhelmingly relentless nature of this new social contract. The baby takes. The parent gives. End of story. What startles many couples is the excruciating toll it can take on their quality of life - especially their marriages." [3]

Having children increases stress due to things like:

- Lack of sleep

- Increased chores

- Decreased personal time

- Needing to set limits on children's behavior

Children add stress to their parent's relationship.

Babies and preschoolers certainly need plenty of adult help.

Differences between How Men and Women Handle Stress

Men and women respond differently to stress. In his book Why Mars and Venus Collide: Improving Relationships by Understanding How Men and Women Cope Differently with Stress, Dr. John Gray explains "Men tend to shift gears, disengage, and forget their problems, while women are compelled to connect, ask questions, and share problems. This simple distinction can be extremely destructive in a relationship if it is not appreciated and respected." [4]

The physical differences between men and women's brains contribute to the differences in how each handles stress. When men are stressed their testosterone levels drop and doing something relaxing like reading, watching TV or napping helps rebuild their testosterone.

On the other hand, when women are stressed, their oxytocin levels fall. Talking about the problem and receiving messages of caring, understanding and respect rebuilds that oxytocin in women.

Men tend to get quiet under stress and retreat to their caves to recover. Women often seek out others to talk to about their stress. Appreciating these differences in handling stress can help couples better understand each other and provide the support the other one needs.

Working Better Together Under Stress

When there's a problem you need to discuss with your partner, it's best to have this discussion when you are both calm. If you are upset, the thinking part of your brain is significantly hampered by the chemicals released in your brain from this upset.

Once you are ready to discuss an issue with your spouse or partner, it helps to say things in ways that don't make the other person defensive. Gray gives several examples of what to say that will either make things better or worse.

For example, instead of saying "That doesn't make any sense." Gray suggests responding "OK, let me make sure I understand you. Are you saying ..." Instead of claiming "You are getting upset over nothing." say "I know this is upsetting. Are you saying ...?"[5]

Gray provides many recommendations for how to approach discussing problems in ways that are more likely to have positive results. He even provides ways to respectfully take a time out if the conversation is getting heated. He suggests saying "What you say is important to me. I need some time to think about this and then we can talk." rather than "This is a complete waste of my time. I can't talk with you."[6]

What works best to help you handle stress? What helps your partner?

_____

_____

Pulling Together as a Family with Weekly Family Meetings

When times are tough, one of the worst feelings is that you are all alone. Believing that nobody else really knows what you are going through and that you must figure it out yourself weighs heavily.

Kids need help getting through challenging times and so do parents! It can be easy to miss that one of your family members is struggling.

One of the best things you can do to prevent these feelings of isolation is to have regular, planned opportunities to communicate. Family meetings are a way to make this happen.

Weekly family meetings help keep the lines of communication open.

Holding Family Meetings

Weekly meetings provide a structure for regularly communicating. Pick a day of the week that works best. It might be Sunday evenings so you can get on the same page for the upcoming week. Perhaps a Thursday or Friday night works better. The important thing is to pick a day and time that your family can commit to setting aside every week.

These meetings should be short – 30 minutes works well. This means there will only be time for a few agenda items and the rest will have to wait until the following week.

Everyone can have a role in the family meeting. Some of the roles you might want include:

- Agenda Keeper – reads the agenda and sticks to it

- Note Taker – records what is discussed and decided

- Time Tracker – keeps track of time for each item and announces when it's time to move on

- Fun Activity Organizer – plans fun activity to end the meeting

Family meetings are a chance for everyone to be heard. This is not a time for lecturing by parents. It's a time to pull together as a family to figure out how to support each other.

Creating the Agenda

You can put a piece of paper on the refrigerator or a bulletin board where anyone can add agenda items. For example, if your kids complain that they are too rushed in the mornings, you can ask them to put that on the agenda.

Setting a positive tone at the beginning of the meeting is important. You can do this by first deciding who will have each role in the meeting. Next provide time for noticing what is going well and giving compliments.

Your agenda might look something like this:

- Who has each role? Agenda Keeper, Note Taker, Time Tracker, Fun Activity Organizer
- Compliments. What's going well?
- Update on last meetings' action items
- Topic 1: Sharing the bathroom in the morning
- Topic 2: Keeping the front entry way clean
- Topic 3: Our schedule for next week
- Fun activity

Often one of the agenda items is the schedule for the upcoming week. Knowing who must be where and when is critical for busy families!

Looking For Solutions

Agenda items will often involve a problem one member is experiencing. For example,

- When Mom comes home from work, the house feels chaotic.
- Dad would like more help in preparing and cleaning up from meals.
- One child feels stressed due to being rushed in the mornings.
- The dog is not getting out for a walk every day.
- There are shoes and jackets all over the front entry way.
- The kids are hungry when they get home from school and can't find snacks.

After stating the problem, the next step is to brainstorm possible solutions. Write down all the ideas. This is not the time to judge whether the ideas will work, just write them down.

Once you've thought of some possible solutions, circle the ones that meet everyone's needs. Let the person who brought up the problem choose which idea to try first. Discuss how it's working in next week's meeting. If the solution is not working well, choose a different option.

Taking Notes

Keep notes from your family meetings. By writing down the decisions you make, you'll be able to come back to them the following week to see how it's going. You may need to tweak some of your solutions if they aren't quite solving the problem.

It's easy to forget what you have committed to trying if it's not written down. This is also an opportunity for everyone to agree on what was decided. Putting each weeks' notes in a notebook or folder will allow you to look back and see how far you've come!

Scheduling Your First Meeting

You could make the first meeting an introduction to the concept of meeting – having someone taking notes, having an agenda, keeping track of time and planning something fun for the end of the meeting.

Explain how family meetings can help everyone solve problems and keep the household running smoothly. Let everyone know how to add items to the agenda. End with something enjoyable like a quick game, song, treat or story.

Kids thrive on schedules and certainty. Weekly family meetings provide consistency for addressing problems and finding solutions. Life is so much better when you feel "we're all in this together"!

When is the best time for your family to meet?

_____

Identifying Your Family's Top 5 Moral Values

What are your deepest held moral values? How are you teaching these values to your children? Are you doing it alone or are you seeking help from religious organizations or other resources?

Teaching your kids moral values is one of the most important responsibilities you have as a parent. For your children to act morally, they need to know the good, care about the good and practice doing the good.

The way your kids choose to treat others is critical. There are too many news stories of children committing suicide due in part to the cruel behavior of other kids. There are too many kids posting mean comments on social media. Too many kids avoiding activities due to bullying. How do you guide your kids in treating others?

Knowing the Good

What does it mean to be a good person? What traits does your family most value? Renée Trudeau, author of <u>Nurturing the Soul of Your Family</u>, shared that when her son was entering middle school they created a "Family Purpose Statement". She described they "highlighted the top five qualities that were most important to us. At the top of our list: compassion - for self and for others."[7]

What virtues make your family's top five list? Some to consider include:

Acceptance: having an objective attitude toward other's ideas and practices that differ from your own

Compassion: understanding the suffering of others or self and wanting to do something about it

Courage: willingness to do difficult things

Equality: believing everyone deserves equal rights and to be treated with respect

Fairness: acting in a just way, sharing appropriately

Generosity: willingness to give resources, help or time to others

Honesty: being truthful and sincere

Integrity: sticking to your moral and ethical principles and values

Kindness: being considerate and treating others well

Perseverance: persisting in a course of action, belief or purpose

Politeness: using good manners, acting in socially acceptable ways

Respect: showing consideration for the worth of someone or something

Responsibility: being reliable in your obligations

Self-control: staying in control of your words and behavior

One way to help your children internalize these characteristics is to notice them. When you see your child being responsible, honest or showing compassion, comment on it. For example, if your child attempts to comfort a child who is hurt, you can say "That's kind of you to help him."

Caring About the Good

There is a big difference between knowing about moral values and trying to adopt the traits. Often standing up for your morals takes courage and strength.

After your family has selected your top five values, find examples of how you've demonstrated those in the past. Your kids may want to create a poster for each value with pictures and examples of that value. Leave space to add more examples.

Next encourage each person commit to one value they want to focus on for the week. Check in daily with each other to see if there was an opportunity to act on that value. What happened? How did it feel? What did you learn?

Asking your kids these questions sends the message that you care about these values. Like adults, your kids will make mistakes and act in ways that don't represent their highest values. When this happens, help them find a way to make amends. Ask questions to guide your kids in figuring out what they would like to do to make things better.

Thinking Before Acting

Your kids will have daily opportunities to choose to act on their values. Behaving ethically requires a strong moral conviction.

It's not always easy to stay in control of your words and actions. My son's cross-country coach taught the kids to THINK before they speak or act by considering:

- T - Is it true?
- H - Is it helpful?
- I - Is it inspiring?
- N - Is it necessary?
- K - Is it kind?

This simple acronym helps kids pause to consider the impact of their words and actions beforehand.

Taking Action That Support Your Values

There are times in our lives when we are shaken to our core. The very foundation of our lives seems to be at risk. It may be triggered by things like political upheaval, health issues or relationship problems.

These situations produce strong emotions. You may feel furious, perplexed, distraught, alarmed or apprehensive. When something you deeply care about is at risk, you experience stress.

When you positively embrace stress, it propels you to act in alignment with your values. You feel like you must act to maintain your integrity. You can no longer sit back and watch what is happening.

Stress can energize you to take positive action. In her book, The Upside of Stress, Kelly McGonigal explains "The energy you get from stress doesn't just help your body act; it also fires up your brain. Adrenaline wakes up your senses. Your pupils dilate to let in more light, and your hearing sharpens. The brain processes what you perceive more quickly. Mind-wandering stops, and less important priorities drop away. Stress can create a state of concentrated attention, one that gives you access to more information about your physical environment."[8]

McGonigal is describing an immediate physical response to a stressful situation. These concepts also apply to prolonged stressful situations.

Stress energizes and focuses you in various ways:

- Your senses are awakened. You are no longer sleepwalking through the situation.

- Your priorities come into sharp focus. Things that are trivial simply fall away.

- Your attention is concentrated on the situation.

- You recognize information that you were previously ignoring.

This focused energy motivates you to act. Ideally the action you choose is in alignment with your highest values.

Harnessing Stress To Do Good

Your moral character is revealed by the actions you choose to take or to avoid. Do you choose to take the high road or the low road?

Most of us fantasize about some low road options. While these options produce temporary feelings of getting some justice or revenge, ultimately they do not serve us well.

Your emotions are always OK – there are not right and wrong emotions. However, how you choose to behave in response to your emotions may or may not be OK.

So what can you do to take the high road? What can you encourage your kids to do with their strong emotions?

Acting is critical to owning your power and helping your kids own their power. What is one thing you can do to help the given situation? If you are not sure what options are available, try a couple internet searches on your topic. You may want to join a group of like-minded people with whom you can work together to create the changes you are seeking.

Jacqueline Way wanted to help her 3-year-old son Nic learn to be generous and create positive change. She thought this was equally as important as learning to tie his shoes or brush his teeth. Jacqueline and Nic decided to do one thing a day to give back to the world.

They found simple ways to give back that Nic could do. They decided to record and share what they did each day. After doing this for a year, they wanted to encourage others to join in so they started 365give.

You can find inspiring ideas for giving and join for free on their site 365give.ca.

While your children will have many influences on their moral development, you play the biggest role. You are their first teacher. They look to you to learn how to act in the world.

What are your family's top five moral values?

1. _____
2. _____
3. _____
4. _____
5. _____

What are some ways your family practices these values?

_____
_____
_____
_____

Responding to Kids with Compassion Instead of Criticism

Critical comments flow easily for most parents. In fact, it may be so natural that you don't even notice yourself making negative comments.

When you criticize your kids, you are usually trying to correct their behavior or help prevent them from making mistakes. While these are worthwhile goals, what if criticism does more harm than good?

Criticizing Kids Teaches Them to Be Self-Critical

A big problem with criticism is that kids tend to quickly internalize it and then repeat it back to themselves. When your kids use negative self-talk, they hold themselves back instead of confidently moving forward.

Your kids quickly internalize your criticism.

In her book Self-Compassion: Stop Beating Yourself Up and Leave Insecurity Behind, Dr. Kristin Neff writes "When mothers or fathers use harsh criticism as a means to keep their kids out of trouble ("don't be so stupid or you'll get run over by a car"), or to improve their behavior ("you'll never get into college if you keep getting such pathetic grades"), children assume that criticism is a useful and necessary motivational tool. Unsurprisingly, research shows that individuals who grow up with highly critical parents in childhood are much more likely to be critical toward themselves as adults.

People deeply internalize their parents' criticisms, meaning that the disparaging running commentary they hear inside their own head is often a reflection of parental voices – sometimes passed down and replicated throughout generations." [9]

Think back to how your parents spoke to you when you were growing up. Do you still hear some of the things they said running through your head? Are those thoughts loving reminders of how amazing you are or are they criticisms? Having self-critical thoughts isn't exactly the legacy you want to give your kids!

Criticism Comes Easier Than Forgiveness or Compassion

Being critical of your children's behavior stems from a belief that criticism is necessary in helping them grow up well. When you criticize your kids, you are attempting to exert control over their behavior to improve it. Is there a better way to do this?

Dr. Kelly McGonigal's research on willpower has found that forgiveness and compassion are more powerful than criticism. In her book, The Willpower Instinct: How Self-Control Works, Why It Matters, and What You Can Do To Get More of It, McGonigal explains "As soon as I mention self-forgiveness in class, the arguments start pouring in. You would think I had just suggested that the secret to more willpower was throwing kittens in front of speeding buses. 'If I'm not hard on myself, I'll never get anything done.' 'If I forgive myself, I'll just do it again.' 'My problem isn't that I'm too hard on myself – my problem is that I'm not self-critical enough!' To many people, self-forgiveness sounds like excuse-making that will only lead to greater self-indulgence."[10]

According to McGonigal, "Study after study shows that self-criticism is consistently associated with less motivation and worse self-control. It is also one of the single biggest predictors of depression, which drains both 'I will' power and 'I want' power. …

Surprisingly, it's forgiveness, not guilt that increases accountability. Researchers have found that taking a self-compassionate point of view on a personal failure makes people more likely to take personal responsibility for the failure than when they take a self-critical point of view. They also are more willing to receive feedback and advice from others, and more likely to learn from the experience."[11]

Compassion Works Better Than Criticism

Let's consider a couple situations and compare responding with criticism to responding with compassion.

Suppose your child comes home with a poor math grade, how might you respond?

- Criticism: "That grade is a disgrace. You're not trying hard enough. How will you get anywhere in life if you can't do better than that?"

- Compassion: "Oh, that's not the grade you wanted. What's your plan for improving it?"

What if your child spills a glass of juice?

- Criticism: "Look at the mess you've made! You need to be more careful!"

- Compassion: "Oops! Let's get a rag so you can clean it up."

If you were the child in these situations, how would each response make you feel?

Neff explains why compassion is more effective than criticism, "So why is self-compassion a more effective motivator than self-criticism? Because its driving force is love not fear. Love allows us to feel confident and secure (in part by pumping up our oxytocin), while fear makes us feel insecure and jittery (sending our amygdala into overdrive and flooding our systems with cortisol). When we trust ourselves to be understanding and compassionate when we fail, we won't cause ourselves unnecessary stress and anxiety."[12]

How can you be more compassionate towards yourself? If you want to be more compassionate and forgiving towards your children, start with how you treat yourself.

One mom said she realized that when she is being compassionate with herself, it is much easier for her to also be compassionate with her son. When she is critical of herself, she also is more likely to be critical of him.

Compassionately Supporting Kids Through Heartbreaking Rejection

Compassion is fueled by love. You love your kids and never want to see them hurt. Unfortunately, you cannot prevent your children from experiencing rejection. Whether it's not being selected for a team or not having a date for the dance, feeling rejected is painful.

Your response in these situations can provide a healing salve for your child's wounds or deepen the pain. When you let them know that you value and love them regardless of what has happened, you provide comfort. Knowing they always have your love is a powerful antidote.

Experiencing a Crushing Blow

Trying out for a team takes courage. Unless your child is guaranteed to make the team, there is the risk of failure. Responding when your child makes the team is easy. The difficult part is how you respond when your child does not make the team.

In her book Braving The Wilderness, Brené Brown describes trying out for her high school drill team, the Bearkadettes. Before leaving on a family trip, her parents swung by the school so she could check the board listing who made the team. Her number was not on the list.

She was crushed. She describes what happened next that made her feel even worse. "I walked back to our station wagon and got in the backseat, and my dad drove away. My parents didn't say one word. Not a single word. The silence cut into me like a knife to the heart. They were ashamed of me and for me. My dad had been captain of the football team. My mom had been head of her drill team. I was nothing. My parents, especially my father, valued being cool and fitting in above all else. I was not cool. I didn't fit in."[13]

Her parents silence spoke volumes. Instead of feeling comforted she writes "And now, for the first time, I didn't belong to my family either."

Feeling Alone Versus Feeling Supported

It can be hard to know what to say when your child is suffering. You may feel powerless knowing that there's nothing you can do to change the situation. You don't know what to say so you decide not to say anything.

The problem with silence is that it leaves your children creating their own interpretations. Brown discusses the issues with being silent explaining "Sometimes the most dangerous thing for kids is the silence that allows them to construct their own stories – stories that almost always cast them as alone and unworthy of love and belonging. That was my narrative, so rather than doing high kicks during halftime, I was the girl hiding weed in her beanbag chair and running with the wild kids, looking for my people any way I could. I never tried out for a single thing again. Instead, I got really good at fitting in by doing whatever it took to feel like I was wanted and a part of something."[14]

The last thing you want is for your child to feel all alone in their pain. You can always say something like "I'm so sorry you didn't make the team. I know how much you wanted this." Give your child a hug and let them know you are there for them.

When your children are distraught, they are not in a space where they are ready for a conversation about what happened. After they've had time to calm down, you might mention "I'm proud of you for trying out. You worked hard on the routines and gave it your best."

Helping your child see their positive attributes helps them psychologically heal. Many people tend to beat themselves up in situations like these which causes further injury. Reminding your children of their strengths will help them grow from the experience. You will be guiding them towards self-compassion rather than self-criticism.

Being there for your children is the greatest gift you can give them. They will experience hard times. Being able to count on your love will give them the courage to take risks and grow to be their best.

When your children experience rejection, how might you respond in a way that would feel supportive?

_____

_____

_____

How can you be more compassionate and less critical of your kids?

_____

_____

_____

How can you be more compassionate towards yourself?

_____

_____

_____

Successfully Tackling Difficult Conversations

How do you feel when you need to talk to your child, your child's teacher, your spouse or someone else about a touchy topic? Are you excited to address this important issue or do you feel like running in the opposite direction? Most people feel a significant amount of anxiety when they think about addressing a situation which is emotionally charged and opinions differ.

When approaching a difficult conversation you have three basic options:

1. Choose to ignore it and hope the situation magically gets better.

2. Launch head first into the conversation and handle it poorly.

3. Prepare ahead of time and handle the conversation well.

It takes preparation to handle difficult conversations well.

While it would be great if challenging situations got better on their own, since this rarely happens let's look at how you can prepare to handle the conversation well.

Preparing for the Conversation

You will increase the odds of having a productive conversation if you prepare ahead of time. Begin by considering your motive for having this conversation.

In the book <u>Crucial Conversations Tools for Talking When Stakes Are High</u>[15], the authors identify three important questions to ask yourself when preparing for a crucial conversation:

1. What do you really want for yourself?

2. What do you really want for others?

3. What do you want to avoid?

Answering these questions is key to holding the right conversation and sticking with it even when the going gets tough.

For example, when Mark suspected his son, Jake, was stealing money from his wallet he wanted to discuss it with him. He prepared for the conversation by thinking through his answers to these questions:

1. What do you really want for yourself? Mark wanted to confirm his suspicion that Jake was taking money out of his wallet. If this was true, he wanted to understand why Jake was taking the money without asking. He wanted to be able to trust his son again.

2. What do you really want for others? Mark wanted Jake to feel comfortable asking for what he needed instead of stealing it. He wanted Jake to feel secure enough in their relationship that he could be honest.

3. What do you want to avoid? Mark wanted to avoid seriously damaging his relationship with his son. He did not want to yell at his son.

Thinking through these questions grounded Mark in how he wanted to approach their conversation.

Opening the Conversation

How you open the conversation is critical. It's important to talk tentatively at the beginning since you only know your side of the situation. Mark does not want to begin with an accusation like "I know you've been stealing money from my wallet".

A better way to start is to share the facts. Facts are the least controversial. It's the conclusions you draw from the facts that may or may not be correct.

In Mark's case, although he thinks Jake is taking the money he doesn't know this for sure. Maybe his wife has ran out of cash and took some of out of his wallet. Or perhaps Jake's younger sister has been taking money for her play store. If Mark begins by accusing Jake of taking the money when Jake really did not take the money, his relationship with Jake will be damaged – something he wanted to avoid.

Mark might begin by sharing his facts saying "I'm concerned because there has been money missing out of my wallet lately. What are your thoughts on this?" Jake then had a chance to respond. In this case Jake confessed to taking the money to give it to a classmate as payment for not being bullied. Once Mark understood what was going on, he was able to work with Jake on other options for dealing with the bullying.

Staying in Conversation

When people do not feel safe in a conversation, they turn to fight-or-flight. If you notice that your child is withdrawing from the conversation or getting angry and defensive, it is time to restore your child's feeling of safety.

One way to do this is to clarify what you do and do not intend to be communicating. For example, Jake might have responded to his dad "You always blame me for everything!" Mark could have clarified "I am not trying to blame you. I do want to understand why there is money missing from my wallet."

Another approach to restoring safety is to acknowledge the other person's feelings. Mark might have said "It sounds like you feel angry and misunderstood." The fact that his dad has recognized his feelings is likely to calm Jake down.

If emotions are so hot that holding a reasonable conversation is not possible, then it's wise to take a break to allow time for everyone to calm down. Decide on a time to continue the conversation so that it's clear you are not dropping the topic for good.

Concluding the Conversation

Often a difficult conversation will involve making decisions. It's easy for participants to leave a conversation with very different ideas about the decisions and commitments which were made. You can reduce the possibility of miscommunication by writing down the major points discussed along with any decisions made.

If you've brainstormed ideas for solving the problem, be sure to write those ideas down along with the idea you decided to try first. Figure out when to get together again to review how the plan is working. You can always adjust the plan or try a different idea.

You will certainly have the opportunity for many difficult conversations with your children and others. The better you get at handling these challenging conversations, the more likely you are to enjoy success in your relationships.

What is one difficult conversation that you might have with your child?

Before having the conversation, answer these questions:

1. What do you really want for yourself?

2. What do you really want for others?

3. What do you want to avoid?

Positively Focusing Emotional Energy

Think of a challenging parenting situation which you've been dealing with for a few months or perhaps a few years. It might involve concerns about your child's performance at school, use of digital devices, friendships, lying, negative attitude or use of drugs.

Feeling Emotionally Drained

These unsolved problems can drain you emotionally. When you think about the problem you might find yourself feeling angry, worried or sad. What do you do to feel better? You might distract yourself with a favorite activity or perhaps a large glass of wine. While this does nothing to solve the problem, at least you temporarily feel better.

Serious, unsolved problems are emotionally draining.

Perhaps you try once again to change your children's behavior by talking to them or punishing them. You know this hasn't worked in the past but you don't know what else to do. Maybe you remind yourself that your child is going through a phase which should be over soon.

Parents dealing with ongoing problems describe feeling like being on a roller coaster. They seesaw between feeling OK and feeling terrible. They get pushed from one side to the other by events and their own thoughts.

Laurie first became concerned about her son, Aiden, when he was 10. He came home from a friend's house smelling of smoke. When she questioned him about this he blamed his friend's mom for smoking around him. Laurie knew this woman did not smoke and soon Aiden admitted he had tried smoking with his friend. She grounded him at home for a couple days and he promised never to do it again.

The next big incident happened a couple years later when Laurie picked Aiden up from a party. His words slurred, and he confessed he had been drinking. Laurie told Aiden he could not go to this friend's house again but his friend was welcome to come to their home. Next Aiden's grades started slipping. When she talked to him about his grades, he claimed school had gotten boring but agreed to work harder on turning in all his assignments.

Each time Aiden reassured her that he would change his behavior she felt better. However, it wasn't long before Aiden would have another red flag behavior. She was increasingly feeling angry or worried most of the time.

Choosing Positive Action Feelings

Laurie felt like she was on a pendulum swinging back and forth without making any real progress. She would get angry and punish Aiden. He would apologize. Before long there would be another incident.

She was discouraged because nothing she did seemed to work. Can you relate to having a problem like this? When you are experiencing strong negative feelings like anger or frustration, you cannot do your best thinking.

You can improve your ability to think clearly by first calming down. Next choose the feelings you want to have when trying to solve this problem. Choose three positive feelings that you would like to hold. These are some possibilities:

authentic	balanced	brave	calm	capable
committed	compassionate	competent	confident	courageous
curious	determined	empowered	energized	engaged
fair	focused	grounded	hopeful	inspired
kind	loving	motivated	patient	peaceful
powerful	present	relaxed	vibrant	worthy

Once you choose your three words visualize them in a triangle. Imagine this triangle sitting in your heart area. As you work on the problem, go back to visualizing your triangle of feelings whenever you are being pulled off balance.

For example, Laurie may want to feel curious, empowered and hopeful when she approaches Aiden. She will visualize something like this:

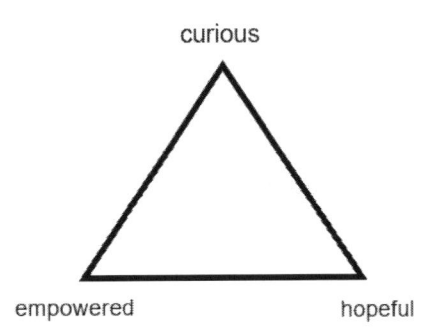

```
             curious
               /\
              /  \
             /    \
            /      \
           /_____\
    empowered      hopeful
```

Keeping these feelings in mind, she realizes she is curious about many things. She does not know what Aiden is going through with his friends, school and sports. What are his biggest worries? What does he do when he feels stressed? Does he see any drawbacks in drinking and using drugs? How does he handle situations where he's uncomfortable with what his friends are doing?

Laurie feels empowered by having this difficult conversation with Aiden. She realizes she cannot change Aiden's behavior but she can change how she approaches him. Previously she was yelling at him and punishing him. This put more distance between them without resolving the underlying problems.

Moving Forward Towards Solutions

Problems that have been going on for a few months or years are going to take time to solve. One good conversation is a healthy start. You will want to connect regularly to keep on top of the problem resolution.

Weekly family meetings are one way to connect with each other regularly. Whatever problems one person in a family is experiencing affects everyone in the family. Pulling together to support each other creates a more loving atmosphere.

During your family meetings you are likely to discuss problems that are causing anger or frustration. Use this opportunity to explain how the triangle of three positive feelings can help. Being able to approach problems from this perspective will increase the likelihood of finding a solution. Take notes so you can look back at the progress your family makes as you solve problems together!

Try this new approach to a challenging parenting situation. Which three feelings would you like to have while dealing with this situation?

_____

Imagine the triangle image in your heart space. Address the problem from this perspective. What shifted or changed for you?

_____

_____

_____

Recognizing Red Flag Behaviors - Clues Kids Aren't Coping Well

Experiencing stress is part of growing up. What happens when children feel overwhelmed by stress? If your child is under age six, the result is often a tantrum. They aren't trying to misbehave. They simply have not developed better coping skills.

Older kids may also have meltdowns when they are flooded with strong feelings. They are developing better coping skills but may not have the presence of mind to use those skills.

All kids experience stress. Some turn to talking to friends while others try escaping with drugs. How are your kids coping with their stress?

Developing Healthy Coping Strategies

Your kids may feel pressure to do well at school, sports and other activities. They also have various social pressures with classmates, friends and family.

Since all kids need to handle stress, developing healthy coping strategies is important. What do your kids like to do to calm down? Some healthy ways kids cope with stress include:

- Drawing or coloring
- Listening to music
- Playing an instrument
- Meditating
- Talking to someone
- Exercising or going for a walk
- Writing in a journal
- Practicing a sport
- Playing with a cat or dog

Everyone needs healthy coping strategies for handling stress

Ideally your children have many healthy coping skills to choose from. Establishing a daily practice for dealing with stress is helpful.

Recognizing Unhealthy Coping Behaviors

When your kids are overextended or exhausted, their coping skills may start to crumble. Even though they were coping well a few days ago, they may not be able to do it today.

Some behaviors indicate potentially serious problems in coping with stress. It's natural to want to minimize the possible consequences and hope that things will get better. Don't all teens act like this? Isn't this a phase that will soon pass?

What behaviors may indicate a problem? Red flag behaviors include:

- Spending less time interacting with your family
- Not sleeping well
- Acting secretively
- Eating lots of junk food or seriously restricting eating
- Spending increasingly significant time on digital devices
- Falling grades
- Sexually inappropriate behavior
- Getting caught drinking or using drugs
- Being suspended from school
- Inflicting self-harm

A red flag behavior is any behavior that makes you concerned about what's going on with your child. When you get a gut feeling something isn't right, take it seriously.

A grandma wrote me concerned about "an almost perfect grandson". When I asked about why this is a problem, she explained "He is 16 and suddenly not talking much at all at home. He is so admired at school (class Vice President) and sports. Coaches and teachers write letters home praising him. Other parents keep telling their kids they want them to be more like Zack. He is involved in sports and everything at school and I feel he has a lot of pressure set upon him. Not sleeping well but his plate is full."

It sounds like Zack might feel pressure to "be perfect". Not sleeping well is a red flag. It's also a red flag that he's not talking as much at home.

She described Zack's parents as loving parents who are very involved in their kids' lives. However, they also are dealing with their own issues in counseling. She was concerned that Zack was keeping his problems to himself so as not to further burden them. Knowing about kids in Zack's school who had died from suicide added to her worries.

Suicide is the second leading cause of death for kids and youth ages 5 to 24-years-old[16]. Reducing suicide among kids involves acting on these red flags before it's too late.

Raising Your Concerns

When you feel like something isn't right with your child but don't know what's wrong, you need more information. Discussing it with your child in a non-threatening way is a good first step. Find a time alone when neither of you feels rushed. It may be easier to talk while walking or enjoying a bowl of ice cream.

It takes courage to have difficult conversations. You may feel like you don't know what to say. Begin by stating a fact and asking an open-ended question.

For example, pretend your child hasn't been sleeping well the past few nights. You're concerned there's something going on that's upsetting your child and making it hard to sleep. Your conversation might start like this:

You: "I noticed you haven't slept well for the past couple nights. Why do you think that is?"

Child: "I don't know."

You: "I'm concerned you're stressed about something that's getting in your way of sleeping."

Child: "You worry too much."

You: "Maybe ... and it's because I love you so much!"

Child: "Well I'm fine."

You: "I want to believe you are fine but I feel like something isn't quite right. Last night you were quiet at dinner and then immediately went back into your room."

Since you are concerned enough to bring this up, you don't just want to drop it when your child claims to be fine. In this last statement, you've added another fact that bothers you.

At this point, your child may offer some information about what is going on. You cannot force your child to talk. If your child doesn't want to discuss it with you, another option is to set up an appointment with a counselor or other trusted adult.

By starting the conversation, you've shown your child you care deeply and will talk about difficult subjects. If your child is struggling with serious problems, getting professional help is wise. Plan to follow up with regular conversations. Acting when you notice red flags sends a strong message that you are there to help your children through life's challenges.

What healthy ways do your kids have for coping with stress?

_____

_____

_____

Are there any red flag behaviors you have noticed?

_____

_____

_____

Reducing Suicide Among Kids

You love your kids. The last thing you want to think about is that your child might die from suicide.

Is there anything you can do today to prevent a tragedy like this from happening? Some parents who have suffered the devastating loss of their child to suicide are working hard to prevent it in other families.

Talking About Depression and Suicide

John and Susie Trautwein lost their 15-year-old son, Will, to suicide. Will is the oldest of their four children. In John's book, My Living Will: A Father's Story of Loss & Hope[17], he describes their families' fun, loving home. The night Will hung himself they had no indication he was depressed let alone suicidal.

Will was doing well in school and sports plus had plenty of friends. It's hard to imagine that kids like Will would feel like ending their lives. Yet it happens.

Michael Phelps, Olympic swimmer and winner of 28 medals, has struggled with depression since his teens. In the MSN article titled "Michael Phelps: 'I am extremely thankful that I did not take my life'"[18] Phelps reports falling into major depression after every Olympics. He finally reached out for help when he hit an all-time low where he wasn't eating or sleeping well and didn't want to be alive.

The article quotes Phelps saying, "I was very good at compartmentalizing things and stuffing things away that I didn't want to talk about, I didn't want to deal with, I didn't want to bring up -- I just never ever wanted to see those things." After learning to talk about his feelings, he reports life was much easier.

Recognizing Boys' Vulnerable Feelings

Males are 3.5 times more likely to die from suicide than females. Part of what puts them at higher risk is society's expectations of males.

Brené Brown discussed her research on shame in an interview with Krista Tippet titled "The Courage to Be Vulnerable"[19]. Brown reported "For men, there's a really kind of singular, suffocating expectation and that is do not be perceived as weak." These expectations are woven into the fabric of our society. At a high school football game, the

Marines at the recruiting table wore shirts that said, "Pain is weakness leaving the body".

If males are not supposed to show any weakness, what do they do with feelings like fear, disappointment or sadness? Some turn these emotions outward expressing them as anger or aggression. Others turn these emotions inward criticizing themselves. Both choices bury the underlying vulnerable emotions.

How can boys be helped to deal with their difficult feelings? Some schools have created safe groups where boys can share their struggles. The Seattle Times article "Despondent Seattle teen found a future through film; now he's giving back"[20] describes how a group like this helped Vannady Keo.

"As a freshman at Kentlake High School, Keo was struggling with depression, not doing well at school and at odds with his Cambodian-born parents.

'I was just a typical American kid. My parents wanted me to have Cambodian roots, so those were some things we argued about,' Keo said. 'In school I always had a lot of friends. I would always try and hide my depression by hanging out with them, being the cool kid, the class clown.'"

Things changed for Keo when he joined the Southeast Asian Young Men's group. The group met weekly to discuss common experiences of feeling isolated, depressed and disconnected from their parents. Keo said sharing his problems helped him realize he wasn't alone.

Realizing you aren't alone is healing for both boys and girls. Even if you don't think your kids would consider suicide, talk to them about it. By starting a conversation, you let them know you can handle hearing about their difficulties. Hopefully knowing there are people they can turn to for help will prevent them from turning to suicide as a solution.

Talk to your kids about suicide if they are old enough. Where would they turn for help if they were seriously struggling? Let them know they can always call the Suicide Hotline: 1-800-SUICIDE

Following Your Parenting Intuition

Do you ever feel confused and torn when trying to figure out what is best for your kids? It might be around choosing a school, a sports team, a summer camp or someone to watch them. Do you find yourself thinking and re-thinking the pros and cons of each choice only to feel even more uncertain?

Struggling with conflicting feelings is a sign to pause and reflect before acting. Most often this struggle happens when you are trying to convince yourself of an answer or solution that is somehow not right.

Trust your intuition.

Recognizing Your Intuition

You are probably an expert at logically explaining your decisions. This is what you learned in school – don't just write down an answer, you need to be able to explain your answer. Intuition is about knowing the right answer in your gut even though you can't easily explain it.

For example, Steve was concerned about his son's relationship with his stepfather. He described some awkwardness when picking his son up from his mother's house, a previous incident involving Child Protective Services, his son's inappropriate touching behavior and many other details.

Steve's gut feeling was that his son was being sexually abused by the stepfather. He didn't want to believe this so he questioned his conclusion. While he couldn't prove it with hard evidence, he knew that the fear he felt for his son's safety was legitimate. He decided to act to protect his son based on his intuition.

Another example involves my mom and brother. My mom noticed that my 10-year-old brother was limping. She took him to the doctor and they took an x-ray of his leg. The doctor didn't find anything wrong and told her that she was just being over-protective.

He continued to limp. Her gut feeling told her something was wrong so she took him to a different doctor. That doctor saw the x-rays and immediately recognized there was a problem with his left hip joint. He had Perthes Disease which was causing the joint to deteriorate.

It was important that he took the weight off that joint as soon as possible to reduce further damage. After wearing a brace for a couple years, the joint completely healed. Trusting her gut instead of the first doctor's advice saved my brother from permanent damage.

Tapping Into Your Intuition

Listening to your intuition isn't easy. In his book <u>The Gift of Fear</u> Gavin de Becker says "We think conscious thought is somehow better, when in fact, intuition is soaring flight compared to the plodding of logic. ... Intuition is the journey from A to Z without stopping at any other letter along the way. It is knowing without knowing why."[21]

If you've ever said "I just knew" without knowing how you knew, you've used your intuition. Your intuition can pull together the millions of bits of information your brain collects every day into "the truth".

Does this sound too mysterious or weird? de Becker writes "It may be hard to accept its importance, because intuition is usually looked upon by us thoughtful Western beings with contempt. It is often described as emotional, unreasonable, or inexplicable. Husbands chide their wives about 'feminine intuition' and don't take it seriously. If intuition is used by a woman to explain some choice she made or a concern she can't let go of, men roll their eyes and write it off. We much prefer logic, the grounded, explainable, unemotional thought process that ends in a supportable conclusion. In fact, Americans worship logic, even when it's wrong, and deny intuition, even when it's right.

Men, of course, have their own version of intuition, not so light and inconsequential, they tell themselves, as that feminine stuff. Theirs is more viscerally named a 'gut feeling'."[22]

Whether you call it intuition or a gut feeling, everyone has access to this source of wisdom. How can you become more in tune with your intuition? Take time to just be still. When you are quiet it is easier to hear what your gut is trying to tell you.

What do you feel at your core is the right decision? Go with that even if you can't rationalize exactly why it's the best choice. Your gut feelings will steer you in the right direction.

What is an example of a parenting situation where you trusted your intuition?

_____

_____

_____

Habitually Responding in Helpful Ways to Parenting Situations

You are bombarded with making many parenting decisions every day. From deciding what to serve for dinner to responding to your children when they don't want to eat what you've made, you're continually assessing situations and making choices.

Primarily these are little responses, small decisions that you make multiple times each day. How much does any single response matter? Generally not much, but it's the accumulation of all these little responses that create your family culture.

Assessing Your Current Habits

Step back for a moment and pretend you are an invisible stranger observing your family. What do you see? Where is the most tension? Do you hear a lot of yelling? What happens when the children misbehave? How do disagreements between children get resolved?

Establishing good parenting habits makes dealing with challenging kids' behavior easier.

When you look at your current family environment, what do you see is working well? If you could change a couple things, what would they be?

Creating Habits for Challenging Situations

When you go to Starbucks, you are expecting a pleasant experience in return for paying a premium price for their coffee. Have you ever noticed that their employees maintain their friendly, cheerful attitude even when it's hectic? How do they do this?

In his book The Power of Habit, Charles Duhigg explains "Starbucks has dozens of routines that employees are taught to use during stressful inflection points. There's the *What What Why* system of giving criticism and the *Connect, Discover, and Respond* system for taking orders when things become hectic." [23]

When things get difficult, Starbucks employees fall back on these routines. Duhigg writes, "This is how willpower becomes a habit: by choosing a certain behavior ahead of time, and then following that routine when an inflection point arrives."

Similarly, while you can't be prepared for every parenting situation, the healthy habits you've developed can guide you through the toughest situations. For example, if you are extremely angry because of your children's behavior, your habit might be to say something like "I'm too upset right now to talk to you. Let's both go to our rooms and cool down. We'll discuss it after that."

Developing Good Parenting Habits

Your habits and your children's habits interact. If your kids don't listen to you until you are yelling, you've established the habit of talking louder and louder until they finally respond. If your children typically beg for things at the store, this habit has paid off for them.

For example, if you want your children to listen to you the first time you make a request then you want to be in the habit of ensuring this happens. So if you ask your child to put his backpack in his room and he ignores you, you may decide to place your hand on his shoulder and gently guide him to putting his backpack away.

Once you've established good parenting habits, responding to your children's behavior becomes much easier. By developing and practicing your behavior, you will be ready to respond in a thoughtful way when your children say things like

- "I don't want to eat that."

- "She's touching me!"

- "Why do I have to go to bed?"

- "Can I watch just one more show?"

- "May I go over to Sam's house?"

You won't have to spend a lot of time thinking about how to respond – you will just do what you always do in these situations. Whether it's your children begging you for something at the store or pleading for a later bed time, you'll know how to respond.

What new parenting habits would you like to establish?

_____

_____

Conclusion

I prefer the saying "practice makes better" to "practice makes perfect" especially when it comes to parenting. There are no perfect parents and trying to achieve some type of perfection often leads to feelings of inadequacy.

Your kids will give you plenty of opportunities to practice your parenting skills. If you regret how you handled a situation, you can always apologize and try a better approach the next time.

Ideally you want to parent in a way that helps your children develop good moral characteristics like honesty, responsibility, self-reliance, kindness, cooperation and self-control. As most parents will readily admit, this is much easier said than done!

How exactly do you parent in a way that brings these characteristics out in your children? Hopefully you've gotten some helpful ideas from this book. Parenting is a long journey which is more fun when you know how to successfully navigate through the twists and turns.

I wish you all the best in your parenting and leave you with this quote:

"I have come to the frightening conclusion that I am the decisive element. It is my personal approach that creates the climate. It is my daily mood that makes the weather.

I possess tremendous power to make a life miserable or joyous. I can be a tool of torture or an instrument of inspiration. I can humiliate or humor, hurt or heal.

In all situations, it is my response that decides whether a crisis will be escalated or de-escalated and a person humanized or dehumanized.

If we treat people as they are, we make them worse. If we treat people as they ought to be, we help them become what they are capable of becoming."

— Johann Wolfgang von Goethe

About the Author

Kathy Slattengren, M.Ed., has helped thousands of parents from across the United States to Australia through online classes, presentations, coaching and books. Her desire is to help you create the family of your dreams. She loves hearing stories about the positive changes parents have made in their families.

Parenting seems intuitive ... until it's not! She and her husband benefited from taking parenting classes when their children were young. Learning how to calmly handle their children's challenging behavior made their family run much smoother. She's dedicated to sharing these successful, research-based ideas with all parents.

Following her passion to help parents and children, she founded Priceless Parenting in 2007. Prior to having her own kids, she took care of abused children while their parents attended Parents Anonymous® meetings. She also worked with runaway teens and their parents. Witnessing these painful consequences fueled her desire to help families thrive instead of struggle.

Her schooling includes a Master of Education degree from the University of Washington and a bachelor's degree in Psychology and Computer Science from the University of Minnesota. This background has enabled her to pull together parenting research into materials that are easy to understand and apply. Kathy lives in Seattle, Washington.

You can keep up with Priceless Parenting ideas by signing up for the free monthly newsletter. Each month focuses on a common parenting challenge incorporating stories from real parents along with suggestions for applying the information to your own family. Sign up for the newsletter at

http://www.PricelessParenting.com

You can join the conversation by participating in Priceless Parenting's Facebook page:

http://www.facebook.com/PricelessParenting

Index

advising, 15
allowance, 130
analyzing, 15
anxiety, 112
approval, 41
asking once, 91
begging, 63, 72
belonging, 121
boundaries, 146
Bravery Ladder, 114
bribing, 63
bullying, 73, 154, 166
Challenging Behavior Worksheet, 78
choices, 27
chores, 27, 127, 130
Collaborative & Proactive Solutions, 84
commands, 28
compassion, 35, 159
complaining, 125
compliance, 96
consequences
   logical, 82
   natural, 81
   reflecting on behavior, 79
control, 25
cool down time, 99
coping strategies, 171
creativity, 136
criticizing, 15, 159
difficult conversations, 164, 170, 173
disappointment, 82
discipline, 58
disrespectful behavior, 22
diverting, 15
emotions, 94, 105, 107
empathy, 33, 94
entitlement, 72
expectations, 98
family meetings, 151
fear, 112
feelings, 94, 106, 107, 169
fight-or-flight response, 13
fitting in, 120
friendship skills, 117

getting help, 101
gratitude, 22
habits, 122
hitting, 59, 100
homework, 68
I Statement, 97
ignoring inappropriate behavior, 39, 70
intuition, 177
labeling, 15
leader, 17
lecturing, 15, 66
listening, 14, 91
love, 41
Monkey Mind, 110
moral values, 154
motivation, 44
nagging, 61
negative attention, 38
negative self-talk, 110, 159
ordering, 61, 90
parenting habits, 179
pause-and-plan response, 14
PEACE Process, 29
perfection, 45, 142
persevering, 126
pleading, 64, 95
pornography, 49
positive approach, 19
positive behavior, 38
power struggles, 25, 67
problem solving, 80
promises, 71
punishment, 58
reassuring, 15
rebelling, 27
red flag behavior, 168, 172
rejection, 161
reminders, 89
respect, 21
responsibilities, 31, 62, 124
rules, 100, 132, 134
scaring, 65
school routines, 123
school success, 122

screen time limits, 46
screen time recommendations, 47
self-care, 143
self-control, 42
setting limits, 64, 93, 115
sex education, 48
sexual abuse, 50
shaming, 74
shaping behavior, 86
sharing, 98
sleep recommendations, 116
social skills, 117
solutions to problem behaviors, 83
soul, 40
spanking, 59
spending money, 72, 130
spying, 73
stress, 149, 156, 171
struggling, 125
suicide, 101, 173, 175
tapping, 108
threatening, 65
time together, 52
time-outs, 99
values, 156
yelling, 60

References and Notes

Chapter 1: Guiding and Encouraging Children

[1] McGonigal, Kelly. <u>The Willpower Instinct: How Self-Control Works, Why It Matters, and What You Can Do To Get More of It</u>. Penguin Group, 2011, p. 52.

[2] Suttie, Jill, "How Mindful Parenting Differs From Just Being Mindful" last modified June 13, 2016. https://www.mindful.org/mindful-parenting-may-keep-kids-trouble/

[3] McGonigal, Kelly. <u>The Willpower Instinct: How Self-Control Works, Why It Matters, and What You Can Do To Get More of It</u>. Penguin Group, 2011, p. 37.

[4] Nelsen, Jane. <u>Positive Discipline</u>. New York, NY: Ballantine Books, 2006, p. 247.

[5] Ford, Judy. <u>Wonderful Ways to Love a Child</u>. Boston, MA: Red Wheel/Wiser, 2003, p. 38.

[6] Bailey, Becky. <u>Easy to Love, Difficult to Discipline</u>. New York, NY: HarperCollins Publisher, 2000, p. 206.

[7] Perry, Bruce and Szalavitz Maia. <u>Born for Love: Why Empathy is Essential and Endangered</u>. New York, NY: HarperCollins Publisher, 2010, p.12.

[8] Goleman, Daniel. <u>A Force for Good: The Dalai Lama's Vision for Our World</u>. Bantam, 2015, p. 77.

[9] Perry, Bruce and Szalavitz Maia. <u>The Boy Who Was Raised As a Dog: And Other Stories from a Child Psychiatrist's Notebook: What Traumatized Children Can Teach Us About Loss, Love and Healing</u>. Basic Books, 2007, p. 229.

[10] Goleman, Daniel. <u>A Force for Good: The Dalai Lama's Vision for Our World</u>. Bantam, 2015, p. 76.

[11] Dalai Lama. Facebook post on February 3, 2012. https://www.facebook.com/DalaiLama/posts/10150530881132616

[12] Burnside, Annie. <u>From Role to Soul: 15 Shifts on the Awakening Journey,</u> Wyatt-MacKenzie Publishing, 2014, p. 112.

[13] Pink, Daniel. <u>Drive: The Surprising Truth About What Motivates Us</u>. Riverhead Hardcover, 2009.

[14] Jacobs, Tom, "The Two Faces of Perfection" last modified January 28, 2010. https://psmag.com/social-justice/the-two-faces-of-perfectionism-8137

[15] "Media and Children", American Academy of Pediatrics, last modified October 21, 2016. https://www.aap.org/en-us/about-the-aap/aap-press-room/Pages/American-Academy-of-Pediatrics-Announces-New-Recommendations-for-Childrens-Media-Use.aspx

[16] Lang, Amy. "How To Talk To Kids Who Are Playing Doctor" last modified August 10, 2017. https://birdsandbeesandkids.com/kids-playing-doctor/

[17] Jenson, Kristen A and Poyner, Gail. Good Pictures Bad Pictures: Porn-Proofing Today's Young Kids. Glen Cove Press. 2014.

[18] Jenson, Kristen A and Poyner, Gail. Good Pictures Bad Pictures Jr.: A Simple Plan to Protect Young Minds. Glen Cove Press. 2017.

[19] Casteix, Joelle. The Well-Armored Child: A Parent's Guide to Preventing Sexual Abuse. River Grove Books, 2013, p. 54.

Chapter 2: Parenting Behaviors to Avoid

[1] Bradley, Michael. Crazy-Stressed. New York, NY: American Management Association, 2017, p. 140.

[2] Nelsen, Jane. Positive Discipline. New York, NY: Random House, 2006, p.198.

[3] Corwin, Donna. Give Me, Get Me, Buy Me! Preventing or Reversing Entitlement in Your Child's Attitude. HCI, 2010, p. xv.

[4] Barbaro, Adriana and Earp, Jeremy. "Consuming Kids: The Commercialization of Childhood". 2008.

[5] Brown, Brené. The Gifts of Imperfect Parenting: Raising Children with Courage, Compassion, and Connection. Sounds True, 2013.

Chapter 3: Responding Positively to Misbehavior

[1] Hohlbaum, Christine. S.A.H.M. I Am: Tales of a Stay-at-Home Mom in Europe. Wyatt-MacKenzie Publishing, 2005.

[2] Coloroso, Barbara. Kids Are Worth It! Giving Your Child The Gift Of Inner Discipline. New York, NY: HarperCollins Publisher, 2002, p. 84-85.

[3] Greene, Ross. Raising Human Beings: Creating a Collaborative Partnership with Your Child. Scribner, 2016.

[4] Kazdin, Alan. The Kazdin Method for Parenting the Defiant Child. New York, NY: Houghton Mifflin Harcourt Publishing Company, 2009.

[5] Faber, Adele and Mazlish, Elaine. How to Talk So Kids Will Listen & Listen So Kids Will Talk, 2012, p.164.

[6] Gottman, John, Declaire, Joan and Goleman, Daniel. Raising an Emotionally Intelligent Child. New York, NY: Fireside, 1997, p. 76-80.

[7] Wolf, Anthony. The Secret of Parenting: How to Be in Charge of Today's Kids--from Toddlers to Preteens--Without Threats or Punishment. New York, NY: Farrar, Straus and Giroux, 2000.

[8] Fay, Jim. An Introduction to Love and Logic: How to Discipline Kids without Losing their Love and Respect, 2004, p. 65.

[9] Wolf, Anthony. The Secret of Parenting: How to Be in Charge of Today's Kids--from Toddlers to Preteens--Without Threats or Punishment. New York, NY: Farrar, Straus and Giroux, 2000.

[10] Pediatric Development and Behavior, "What Makes Time-Out Work (and Fail)?" 6/11/2007.

Chapter 4: Building Your Kids' Life Skills

[1] "Professional Athletic Services", accessed May 17, 2018. http://www.drerinshannon.com/ProfessionalAthleticServices.en.html

[2] "Tapping for Kids - Sports - EFT with Brad Yates", accessed May 17, 2018. https://www.youtube.com/watch?v=aEicobnPGQs

[3] Pincus, Donna. Growing Up Brave: Expert Strategies for Helping Your Child Overcome Fear, Stress, and Anxiety, Little, Brown and Company, 2013.

[4] "National Sleep Foundation Recommends New Sleep Times", National Sleep Foundation, last modified February 2, 2015. https://sleepfoundation.org/press-release/national-sleep-foundation-recommends-new-sleep-times

[5] "Alfred Adler: Theory and Application", accessed May 15, 2018. http://alfredadler.edu/about/alfred-adler-theory-application

[6] Perry, Bruce. Brain Development & Learning Conference May 2014 https://www.youtube.com/watch?v=DXdBFFph2QQ

[7] Madorsky Elman, Natalie and Kennedy-Moore, Eileen. The Unwritten Rules of Friendship: Simple Strategies to Help Your Child Make Friends, Little, Brown and Company, 2008.

[8] Brown, Brené. The Gifts of Imperfection: Let Go of Who You Think You're Supposed to Be and Embrace Who You Are. Hazelden, 2010, p. 25.

[9] Duhigg, Charles. The Power of Habit: Why We Do What We Do in Life and Business. Random House, 2012, p. 19.

Chapter 5: Leading Your Family with Your Best Parenting

[1] Brown, Brené. The Gifts of Imperfection: Let Go of Who You Think You're Supposed to Be and Embrace Who You Are. Hazelden, 2010, p. 56.

[2] Trudeau, Renée. Nurturing the Soul of Your Family: 10 Ways to Reconnect and Find Peace in Everyday Life, New World Library, 2013, p. 5.

[3] Medina, John. Brain Rules for Baby: How to Raise a Smart and Happy Child from Zero to Five, Pear Press, 2010.

[4] Gray, John. Why Mars and Venus Collide: Improving Relationships by Understanding How Men and Women Cope Differently with Stress, Harper Perennial, 2008, p. 33.

[5] Ibid., p. 147.

[6] Ibid., p. 157.

[7] "4 Ways To Practice Self-Compassion", Renée Trudeau & Associates, last modified December 5, 2016. http://reneetrudeau.com/2016/12/4-ways-to-practice-self-compassion.html

[8] McGonigal, Kelly. The Upside of Stress: Why Stress Is Good for You, and How to Get Good at It. Avery, 2016, p. 50.

[9] Neff, Kristin. Self-Compassion: The Proven Power of Being Kind to Yourself. William Morrow, 2011, p. 25.

[10] McGonigal, Kelly. The Willpower Instinct: How Self-Control Works, Why It Matters, and What You Can Do To Get More of It. Penguin Group, 2011, p. 147.

[11] Ibid., p. 147-148.

[12] Neff, Kristin. Self-Compassion: The Proven Power of Being Kind to Yourself. William Morrow, 2011, p. 165.

[13] Brown, Brené. Braving The Wilderness: The Quest for True Belonging and the Courage to Stand Alone. Random House, 2017, p. 12.

[14] Brown, Brené. Braving The Wilderness: The Quest for True Belonging and the Courage to Stand Alone. Random House, 2017, p. 15.

[15] Patterson, Kerry; Grenny, Joseph; McMillan, Ron and Switzler, Al. Crucial Conversations Tools for Talking When Stakes Are High, McGraw-Hill, 2011.

[16] "Suicide in Children and Teens", The American Academy of Child and Adolescent Psychiatry, last modified October 2017, https://www.aacap.org/AACAP/Families_and_Youth/Facts_for_Families/FFF-Guide/Teen-Suicide-010.aspx

[17] Trautwein, John. My Living Will: A Father's Story of Loss & Hope. WestBowPress, 2014

[18] "Michael Phelps: 'I am extremely thankful that I did not take my life", Susan Scutti from CNN, last modified January 19, 2018, https://www.msn.com/en-us/sports/more-sports/michael-phelps-i-am-extremely-thankful-that-i-did-not-take-my-life/ar-AAuSwII

[19] "The Courage to Be Vulnerable" interview, Krista Tippett, January 29, 2015, https://onbeing.org/programs/brene-brown-the-courage-to-be-vulnerable-jan2015/

[20] "Despondent Seattle teen found a future through film; now he's giving back", Ryan Blethen from The Seattle Times, January 24, 2018, https://www.seattletimes.com/seattle-news/despondent-seattle-teen-found-a-future-through-film-now-hes-giving-back/

[21] De Becker, Gavin. The Gift of Fear. Dell, 1999, p. 25.

[22] De Becker, Gavin. The Gift of Fear. Dell, 1999, p. 11.

[23] Duhigg, Charles. The Power of Habit: Why We Do What We Do in Life and Business. Random House, 2012.

Made in the USA
San Bernardino, CA
09 September 2018